THE
INSIDER'S GUIDE
TO
BOOK PUBLISHING
SUCCESS

[•]

ERIC KAMPMANN
MARGOT ATWELL

Library of Congress Cataloging-in-Publication Data

Kampmann, Eric.
   The insider's guide to book publishing success / Eric Kampmann and Margot
   Atwell. – First edition.
      pages cm
   Includes bibliographical references.
   ISBN 978-0-8253-0687-7 (pbk.) – ISBN 978-0-8253-0623-5 (ebook)
   1. Publishers and publishing—United States. 2. Authors and publishers—United
   States. 3. Self-publishing—United States. 4. Books—United States—Marketing.
   5. Selling—Books—United States. I. Atwell, Margot. II. Title.
   Z471.K357 2013
   070.5—dc23
   2012033488

For inquiries about volume orders, please contact:

Beaufort Books
27 West 20th Street, Suite 1102
New York, NY 10011
sales@beaufortbooks.com

Published in the United States by Beaufort Books
www.beaufortbooks.com

Distributed by Midpoint Trade Books
www.midpointtrade.com

Printed in the United States of America

Interior design by Jane Perini, Thunder Mountain Design
Cover Design by Zak Deardoff

Contents

"A Journey through the Grassroots" by Charlene
Costanzo
"Blind Faith and Serendipity" by Philip Beard
"The Necessity of Teamwork" by Eric Kampmann

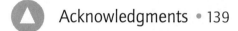

THE
INSIDER'S GUIDE
TO
BOOK PUBLISHING
SUCCESS

Introduction

M any authors think that writing their book is the hardest thing they've ever done. Then they try to publish it. They quickly discover that their work is not even half done.

Book publishing is incredibly complex and requires many skills, such as design, sales, and marketing, not to mention finance. Our aim with this book is to give you a road map to the complex process of publishing, and help you manage all the details that are required to launch your book successfully.

There are many different ways to publish a book. The best choice for you will depend on what you want to achieve by publishing your book. This guide begins with an overview of the publishing options for authors, then describes all the elements that will make up a book's publication, no matter which option you choose. *The Insider's Guide to Book Publishing Success* will take you through the maze of decisions that will be required throughout the process. Of course, we want you to avoid common mistakes, but more importantly, we want to equip you to make the right decisions for your book.

We believe that building a strong team is an essential first step. Most people starting out just do not have the tools to keep all the necessary activities in balance. It takes experience, knowledge, and judgment to maneuver a manuscript through proofreading, cover design, typesetting, marketing, sales, distribution, and finance. As we discuss in the Editorial section, sometimes an author is too close to the material to be able to assess how to edit it. The same holds true throughout the whole process. Having a few talented people you can trust on board can make or break your project. *The Insider's Guide* will describe how to find people for your team and explain how they can make a difference.

The next step is to prepare the product. This is one place where your team can be invaluable. It is great to have an extra set of eyes on the manuscript, cover, jacket copy, and all the other components of the book. It is easy for one person to miss errors or overlook something important. Making every facet of your book great is going to give you a leg up when it comes time to promote it.

After you have prepared your book, it is time to figure out how to sell it: both how to physically sell the book, which might require a distributor, and then how to reach out to your market to excite interest and convince potential readers to buy it. Marketing and publicizing your book can be challenging but it can also be a lot of fun and a great opportunity for you to exercise your creativity. At the same time, it is easy to overspend by "chasing" your market. Sometimes patience and perseverance are the best marketing tools you have at your disposal.

In our experience it is important not to give up on your book prematurely. There is no deadline for when promotion should stop, and sometimes it can take months, or even years, for a book to find its market. Many great success stories start with "For the first six months, nothing happened. But then I started to see more sales..." Don't get caught up in the blockbuster mentality and expect your book to succeed on its publication date. That is unrealistic, and a recipe for disappointment.

This book should give you an overview of the whole process, and the knowledge to make the right decisions for your book. Even if you do not personally engage in every single activity, it is important to have a working knowledge of all the parts of the publishing process. It is our aim to help you increase the odds of success in your favor. We cannot guarantee success but we can take a great deal of mystery out of the publishing process, making the experience more enjoyable and profitable at the same time.

Publishing Overview

I n his novel *A Tale of Two Cities*, Charles Dickens wrote, "It was the best of times, it was the worst of times . . ." Many people look back longingly over the decades and conclude that the best of times for authors has passed us by and that we are dealing with a much more difficult environment today. We do not believe that is true.

Today, more options exist for authors than ever before. As a result, more titles are being published, which has created a whole new set of problems. But here is what authors need to remember: How to publish a book is the author's choice, and in many respects, the method chosen should depend on what the author wants for the book.

In this chapter we outline many viable options open to authors for publishing their books, along with some of the benefits and drawbacks of each method.

Traditional

Traditional publishing is what most people think of when they think of publishing their book. Literary agents are almost always required for most traditional publishers to consider a manuscript. The process of finding a literary agent can be as long and difficult as finding a publisher, but it is pretty much the only way to get a contract with a major publisher.

Once the contract is signed, the publisher does most of the work and the decision-making in bringing the book to market. It controls the process of making the book, selling the book, and marketing the book. It also controls all aspects of the financial arrangement, including how much money it is willing to advance the author, when the royalties will be paid (which is detailed in the contract), and how much money and time it will commit to promoting the book.

But whether an author is working with Macmillan, Random House, HarperCollins, or any other traditional publisher, they can be assured of the company's professionalism and strong market presence. These companies have the ability to reach almost any market in the world, and they have a proven ability to sell a vast number of books. When they are good, they are great. The biggest downside to being published by traditional publishers is that a title can easily get lost in the pack, creating the probability of very disappointing results.

Independent with a Distributor

The phrase "independent publisher" has many meanings depending on who you are talking to. There are many publishers—that are not affiliated with any of the Big Six publishers—like HarperCollins and Random House—that publish books just as well as the big publishers. Many of these independent publishers have niches that they specialize in, such as literary fiction, history and politics, or children's books. Publishers that fall under this category run the gamut from an author publishing his own book under his own imprint to W.W. Norton, a publisher with more than 400 employees.

On the larger and more established end of that range, many publishers still require that agents submit manuscripts to them, or at least prefer it. Independent publishers can be wonderful places for authors, giving them more personal attention than they might get at a bigger publisher. The flip side is that they tend to have less market clout than the bigger publishers.

Distributors are a key element to independent publishers' success. Distributors tend to sell books from many clients so that bookstores and wholesalers buy from one developed relationship rather than many people selling one or a dozen books, giving the client publisher market clout they otherwise could never achieve. There are several companies that provide these distribution services, including Midpoint Trade Books, Perseus, National Book Network, Ingram Publishing Services,

For an author or start-up publisher who wants to create his or her own imprint, there are resources available to help with the process. Midpoint Publishing Services and other similar companies can help with any part of publishing and marketing a book, giving authors and start-up publishers access to professional-level talent in design, editing, and publicity. When working with a consultant or publishing services company, be sure to take a look at samples of other books they have produced to make sure their quality is high.

Partnership

The Partnership Model resembles the Traditional Model in most ways. Here's the difference: rather than getting an advance, the author shares the cost and the income with the publisher. In addition, the author plays a key role in the decision-making process. They are involved with book design and marketing in ways that traditional publishers generally avoid. The real upside here is that the author becomes a player in the publishing process while being supported by a professional publishing infrastructure. Partnership publishers tend to have competitive distribution into mainstream book channels, which is essential if the author wishes to play in the big leagues. While the Partnership Model is not for everyone, it does provide a very credible alternative to the Traditional Model.

Independent/Short Run Strategy

The Short Run Strategy is both a strategy and a type of publishing. It is appropriate in cases where a publisher wants to reach the bookselling market but does not want to invest in a lot of inventory until the book proves itself in the marketplace. With the larger publishers, the system of selling requires that they place the maximum number of copies of a title in the marketplace before a single book has been sold to a consumer. This may work for larger publishers, but it can be a dangerous approach for smaller publishers with limited resources. There is much to admire about traditional publishers, but they often overprint and undersell, creating a situation where capital becomes tied up in slow-selling books.

For many smaller publishers, it can be a better strategy to use "The Long Runway" approach. Most smaller publishers do not have enough money to compete head-to-head with larger publishers. But they do have time on their side. While the larger publishers have fallen into the trap of attempting to make their books succeed immediately, more or less emulating the approach used by Hollywood, the smaller publisher can take the time to build a following for their title, whether through traditional publicity and marketing methods or social networking techniques. The publisher can then go back to press for larger print runs once the book has won attention from readers, which minimizes their risk.

Print-on-Demand (POD)

Print-on-Demand includes a wide spectrum of print-on-demand publishing services that can help authors create a book from a manuscript, print the book in small quantities, and even distribute the book directly through online sales channels. Here are several options:

- **Author Solutions.** Author Solutions is a company that provides basic help for self-publishing authors. Authors can choose from a list of services in the pre-production, production, and marketing fields. In this case, authors can find help with specific publishing tasks, but the big picture is still in the author's hands. Sales and distribution are completely up to the author.

- **Lightning Source**. Lightning Source is a print-on-demand service for self-publishers that is connected to Ingram Publishing Services. Lightning Source can be beneficial because there is no risk of overprinting or paying extra warehouse fees. Because it is connected to Ingram, the book appears in stock and is often printed within twelve hours of the order. The per unit printing costs are considerably higher than a traditional method, however.

- **CreateSpace**. This is a hybrid of Author Solutions and Lightning Source which is owned by Amazon. It offers services like interior review and a cover creator, as well as more in-depth editing, design, and marketing services, but each service is provided at an additional cost. Then, the book is printed with a print-on-demand service and distributed through Amazon, as well as other bookstores and online retailers, at an additional cost. CreateSpace can be good if the author only needs a small amount of help, but the outcome is generally not the most professional or competitive product.

eLaunch

Another option, which we are calling "eLaunch," uses a print-on-demand approach, but with an ebook as the market tester. With this method, the book is published solely as an ebook, which allows the author to gain access to the marketplace at a very low cost and test various marketing strategies to determine which strategy best suits the book. Social networking is often an extremely effective marketing method, since the author can send links to samples of the ebook to their contacts, who can purchase the book with one click. If the book proves to have a market, the files are ready to go to print, and the publisher has an idea of a suitable print number. Having a POD or short-run printer ready to go if the test begins to work is essential for this publishing concept to work best. There are numerous ways for an author to approach this, and services such as MobiPocket and Smashwords can provide a way into the market for authors who are considering this.

Contract

No matter which method the author chooses, there a few key things that must be taken care of. The first of these is negotiating and signing a contract. No matter how comfortable a new author is with legal jargon, consulting a lawyer is always recommended.

The first area on any contract is typically the grant of rights and delineating who owns the copyright of the book. The author should always be in control of the copyright. Then, often deadline dates are included, such as when the work must be delivered by the author, and when the publisher must publish the book. Other key elements (typically not included in contracts with traditional publishers) are the division of production and marketing costs between the author and publisher (or publisher and self-publishing service), and the cost of book purchases for the author. The section addressing author's earnings statements is also important section. This should specify the author's royalty percentage on all the different types of sales (hardcover, paperback, ebook, international rights, book clubs, etc.), when the author will be paid, how the reserve against returns is calculated, and what will happen if there is a negative balance on the account.

Schedule

Once a contract is signed, every book project requires a meticulous schedule in order to keep all the elements on time and all involved parties on the same page. The first date to decide is the publication date. This is the date that books will be available in stores and able to be ordered online. While the specific date does not matter, some seasons are better than others. For instance, if the book is about helping kids with their homework, the back-to-school season would be a good time to publish. Or, if the book is a fun novel, maybe it would fit on summer reading lists. Or would it make a good Christmas present? It is also important to consider big events like national elections that will be hogging publicity during a certain season.

Once a pub date is decided, it is best to work backwards to fill in the rest of the schedule. For books being distributed by a traditional distributor, the books should be off-press six weeks before the pub date. The books should be on press at least four weeks before the off-press date, though the team should consult the chosen printer for a more specific estimate.

The sell-in date is the date that sales representatives will begin previewing the titles to key booksellers. All of the sales materials should be prepared by this date. This is six months before the book will reach retail outlets, though different distributors might need this information earlier or later than others. Some distributors sell on a seasonal method and might need materials earlier in order to produce the seasonal catalog in time. The sample schedule below begins with a polished manuscript. All time frames mentioned depend on length of manuscript, experience level of the team, and time of year.

- Final manuscript is complete.
- Decide on specs (hardcover/paperback, trim size, and ideal length).
- Send manuscript and design suggestions to cover designer.
- Submit manuscript to Library of Congress for CIP data.
- Enter all information onto sell sheet or send to distributor using their preferred method at least six months prior to pub date.
- Send to copyeditor and to interior designer for a sample design. Allow two or three weeks.
- Receive the copyedited manuscript and design. Allow time for the author to go through the suggested changes and any comments or questions from the editor. Also review sample design and relay feedback to the designer. Allow two weeks.
- Send the edited manuscript to the typesetter. Allow two weeks.
- Send typeset manuscript (also known as galleys, or first pass pages) to a proofreader and read through it yourself for any remaining errors. Allow two weeks.
- Send corrections to typesetter. Allow one week.
- Send second proof to indexer and to a proofreader for a slug (or do this yourself). Allow at least two to three weeks for index.
- Send index and any additional changes to the typesetter. This is also when any endorsements, dedication, acknowledgment, and other materials should be included, as well

as all final copyright information and CIP data for the copyright page. Allow one week.

- Finalize the jacket with any endorsements.
- Send final files to the printer. Approve final proofs from printer. Allow four to six weeks for them books to be printed and bound.
- Books ship from the printer. Allow approximately 1 week for them to arrive at the warehouse, and 4-6 weeks until publication date.

Budget

It's no surprise that setting a budget is an important step in the early stages of a book's life. When budgeting a book's pre-production, be sure to allot funds for interior design, typesetting, proofreading, hourly text corrections, cover design, licensing fees for any cover images, and changes to the cover design. Also, budget money for printing Advance Reading Copies (ARCs) if you plan to use them, as well as the ARC cover design. Other pre-production costs include the ebook conversion fee, as well as a production fee if working with an outside production manager. Then, of course, there are the printing costs themselves. When making a budget, it is always smart to round up, and also allow a certain amount for miscellaneous costs that are sure to turn up.

Unfortunately it is nearly impossible to provide sample numbers of expected costs here. The freelancer chosen for each stage of the work, the region the work is done in, and the type and length of the book will affect the numbers dramatically. Before beginning a first budget, it would be worth talking to some designers, typesetters, proofreaders, etc. to get an idea of what they charge and how fast they generally work. For instance, proofreaders can generally complete ten pages per hour, so if a proofreader charges $20 per hour, a total bill of about $512 can be expected for a 256-page manuscript. That said, ask to make sure not just what the rate is, but how hours are calculated, what constitutes an acceptable job, when invoices will be received, and what the payment terms are.

2

Manuscript

....

Importance of Editing

No book should be printed without the advice and assistance
of a good editor. A good editor improves a manuscript through
objectivity and experience and is an invaluable asset for any
writer. A quality editorial process can make a big difference in
the ultimate success of the book. No matter how much editing
has been done by the author or how flawless the author thinks
the manuscript is, an editor is always worth it. Many of the
best books would be unrecognizable without the help of their
editors.

The best way to find a capable editor is by asking other
authors or agents or taking a look at some similar books and
see if an editor is listed in the acknowledgments. Freelance
editors abound, it's just a matter of finding the right one.
Freelance editors can also be found in Literary Market Place™
published by Information Today, Inc. or *The National Directory*

of Editors & Writers for Hire by Elizabeth Lyon. This listing of 600 freelance editors is organized by location across 48 states and is available at Amazon and in bookstores throughout the U.S. Additionally, authors can learn about and stay connected to the industry through the many industry websites and blogs, such as Mediabistro, Bookjobs.com, PW Daily, Publishers Marketplace, and others. Finally, there are a few companies, such as Gotham Ghostwriters, that exist to help authors find ghostwriters and editors. For a fee, they will pair an author with a vetted editor.

When an editor is found, make sure to talk to him or her about what types of books he or she has worked on in the past, and get samples if possible. Also, definitely don't be afraid to call an editor's references. That holds true for any freelancer hired. It's important to make sure that the person chosen does quality work on the schedule he or she puts forth and within the estimate he or she presents for the work. Speaking to people who have worked with the editor under consideration is a good way to ensure that the right person is found for this important job.

Different Types of Editing

■ **Developmental and content.** Developmental and content editing is what shapes the book into a cohesive unit. This stage focuses on structure, overall style, and the big-picture content. Does the voice shift from a disciplined teacher to a joking peer? Does the structure follow the natural train of thought? Is there an aspect of the subject missing that leaves questions unanswered? If the manuscript is fiction, does the main character's personality remain consistent? These are just some of the questions that might be addressed in developmental editing. An editor's feedback is helpful in this stage, because the author may be too close to the work to see the big-picture problems.

- *Line editing.* Line editing is slightly more specific than developmental editing. In this stage, the editor will make sure that every word on the page matches its intent, is the appropriate reading level for the audience, is consistent in style and voice, transitions effectively, and reads smoothly. The line editor is more focused on style while the developmental editor is more focused on story or content.

- *Copyediting.* Copyediting adds another level of specificity, and is usually the final step before the manuscript is set into type. The copyeditor is responsible for correcting all grammar, spelling, and usage errors, as well as making sure the style is consistent. In this case, style refers to a style methodology, like *The Chicago Manual of Style*, which dictates how words, phrases, and typographical elements are used. A good copyeditor is also on the lookout for any phrasing or consistency issues that the line editor may have missed.

ing. The proofreader steps in once the manuscript has been typeset. Since it becomes costly to make
changes once already in the typeset form, the proofreader
is purely responsible for correcting any lingering grammar
and spelling errors as well as typographical errors. Usually
the proofreader is also responsible for noting the correct
page numbers in the table of contents, and double-
checking that all footnotes and endnotes are in the right
place. The first proofreader will read the manuscript
straight from the typesetter in a "cold read." The second
proofreader will do a "slug," which involves checking the
corrected manuscript against the changes requested in order to be sure all changes were caught and no additional
errors were introduced by the typesetter.

■ *Fact Checking.* Not every manuscript requires fact
checking, and good copyeditors or proofreaders will flag
erroneous facts when they see them. However, to ensure
that the book is totally accurate, it can be valuable to hire
a fact checker, especially if there is the possibility of legal
action should some of the facts be incorrect, such as in a
biography or political book.

Jacket Copy and Author Bio

The best way to sell a book in a store is to have the salesper-
son standing next to the consumer telling them all the reasons

the book is great. Unfortunately, this doesn't usually happen. Excellent cover copy is the next best thing to hand selling (convincing, in person, each consumer to buy the book).

Don't let the design get in the way of presenting the sales points. The back cover and flap copy should highlight the most important points that set this title apart from the competition. Use this space to sell the benefits. Excellent endorsement quotes, bullet points, and the author's credentials all help to establish the book's worth in the mind of the consumer.

Remember, the back cover must include the ISBN, bar code, and all other appropriate retail price information. Designers who may not be familiar with book retailing requirements may try to hide or reposition this information so that it doesn't detract from the design. Designer preferences should never take precedence over practical considerations such as positioning the bar code and ISBN on the back outside cover.

The author bio should appear on the back flap in a hardcover, or along the bottom of the back cover in a paperback. The author bio should be brief, but highlight what qualifies the author in their field. Any previous well-known titles might be included. Also, where the author lives should always be included, because marketing and publicity opportunities may arise in their local area.

When an author is instantly recognizable, or will be doing broadcast interviews seen by millions, then an author photo can be a selling point. Family photos from the last vacation have their place, but the author photo should establish credibility. Make sure it conveys information relevant to the text or the authority of the author. Use a current photo—if the photo looks dated, the consumer may jump to the conclusion that the book is dated. If the author is not instantly recognizable or you have limited space, consider putting author information on an "About the Author" page in the back of the book.

Packaging

Packaging is creating the look and feel of the book, as well as all the decisions that will affect how the book is viewed by consumers. Cover design is one major element of packaging, but there are many others. The format, for example: will the book be published as a hardcover or paperback? How big will it to be? What kind of paper will be used? If it's a hardcover, will it have a dust jacket? If it's paperback, will there be French flaps? Should the cover coating be glossy or matte? There are many considerations that seem subtle but will all contribute to how consumers see the book. Many of these distinctions will significantly impact the conclusion potential buyers make about the quality, professionalism, and even the subject matter of the book.

Jacket Design

Good designers are out there waiting to be found just like good editors. Jacket designers are often credited on book jackets, so other well-done covers are the first place to look. Many are independent contractors and might be available for another project, or they can be an excellent resource for networking within the creative community. Use Literary Market Place™, check out The Book Cover Archive online, or ask around; printers might be able to recommend some names.

A professional jacket designer is a key element to creating a professional jacket design, because there is almost magic in creating a design that works. Professional designers will know how to use different fonts, colors, and layout to transform what could be a flyer into a competitive-looking book cover. Designers should be able to provide several design concepts that are unique and allow the publishing team to work from there. Be wary if a designer insists on presenting only one design concept.

One effective method for creating a great cover is to start by looking at the covers of comparable titles. Ideally, the cover will stand out, but in a positive rather than a negative way. See what is standard for the genre and use this as an advantage. Creating a "comparable covers" sheet with other covers in the genre that work well can help lead to what's going to work for this particular book, and give the designer a great jumping-off point.

Interior Design

Interior design can have its share of challenges. Some designers love to experiment with a number of looks or design elements, including different typefaces and font sizes. Common pitfalls include making the interior too busy with clever graphics and many different fonts. Generally, simpler is better. Make sure that the typeface and size are right for the audience. A huge font with large margins wastes space and money when the intended demographic is able to read something smaller. Other pitfalls include choosing a font that's difficult to read, or creating a design that interferes with the reading experience instead of making the book's points and headers more clear.

Typesetting

Often the interior designer will be the typesetter as well. This stage is particularly exciting, because suddenly an ordinary Word® document begins looking like a real book. Be sure to pay close attention, however, and don't get caught up in the excitement and overlook any problems. Make sure all the headings match appropriately, and that bullets, figures, and other special elements are handled fittingly throughout the entirety of the manuscript. It's important not to introduce too many changes once the text is already in this stage. Unnecessary changes become costly extremely fast.

Books are designed in signatures, or sets of pages based on the offset printing process. Signatures are typically 16 pages. Designers must account for this and sometimes add a few blank pages in the back of the book.

Inserts

Sometimes, if there is special material such as photographs or charts, it makes more sense to put it in its own section than to include it throughout the book. The primary reason one would do this would be if high-quality coated paper is required to display images to their best advantage, or if color photographs will be included in a black and white book. A good designer should be able to help with this section, which must be designed and submitted to the printer as a separate file from the rest of the interior.

Inserts are placed according to the signatures of the book, so they may not always appear exactly in the center or perfectly between chapters. When the final trim size and page count is decided, the printer will know the signature breakdown. At that point, it becomes apparent where to place the inserts depending on the breaks between signatures.

Data

- *ISBN (International Standard Book Numbers)*. An ISBN is a 13-digit number that uniquely identifies books and book-like products published internationally, like fingerprints do for people. For more information on the ISBN application process and proper use, go to www.isbn.org. To purchase ISBNs, go to www.myidentifiers.com. If more than one book will be published, it is smart to purchase a group of ISBNs at once, because they will start with the same group of numbers, and it is more cost-effective.

■ *EAN Barcodes.* An EAN barcode is absolutely necessary for the books to be sold anywhere. To use an ISBN to create a bar code, visit www.createbarcodes.com. The best option is the ISBN Bookland EAN, which includes the ISBN and the price within the bar code. The bar code is only scannable if it is at least 80% of the size of the original code, so be sure the cover designer allows enough space. Also make sure that the designer displays it prominently and doesn't try to hide it or alter it in any way.

When creating a bar code, there will be an option to include a printed price or not. Whether or not the price is included is up to the author and publisher.

■ *Library codes.* Cataloging-in-Publication (CIP) Data is a Library of Congress bibliographic record prepared for a title that has not yet been published. The publisher includes the CIP data on the copyright page. The CIP data facilitates book processing for libraries. For more information, visit: www.loc.gov/publish/cip/faqs. Books must be submitted for CIP data at least eight weeks prior to the typesetting stage. Follow the instructions found on the website for tagging the manuscript. Once the CIP data is received, it should be copied directly onto the copyright page, because modifying it slightly will diminish its effectiveness.

- **_BISAC codes._** BISAC codes are another important tool in the bookselling and cataloging environment. Usually, the sales team accepts three separate BISAC codes indicating up to three different genres that the book will be listed under. Ask the distributor for a complete list of their codes. When there are many that would technically fit, choose the codes that give the book the most marketability. These influence the shelves where the book will be found in bookstores.

- **_Index._** An index is an important tool in any non-fiction book. It helps the reader find information quickly and allows anyone to easily go back to the book for additional information or a refresher. The index can also be a good selling tool, as people will often skim the index to be sure that the book includes the information they are looking for.

  Good indexers can be found just like good editors and jacket designers. Indexing is a rather complicated job, so be sure to find a real professional. Anyone being considered should be able to provide references and sample indexes.

  Allow at least two to three weeks after the initial typesetting for the indexer. A minimal index is typically about 5% of the indexable pages, so for a 256-page book, the index would be eighteen pages long.

  If a lot of changes are made to the book after it has been typeset and sent to the indexer, the pagination might change, and it might need to be sent back to the indexer so he or she can check to make sure all the page numbers are still correct. This is yet another reason not to make significant changes at the proofing stage.

Paper Selection

Once a printer is chosen, ask for their paper samples. While most printers have similar standard paper stocks, some printers have slightly different names for them, so it's best to see them in person to be sure.

The paper selection can easily be overlooked, but the decision has a huge effect on the look of the finished book. A thinner paper choice can be appropriate for a longer book to help keep the size down so the book won't intimidate the reader, while a thicker paper can add bulk if the goal is for the book to appear longer or more authoritative. A cream or antique finish can be good for fiction, while white paper is preferable for more serious non-fiction. If the book is in color, glossy or coated paper is an option, but even glossy paper has different thicknesses.

If a very special type of paper is being considered, the publisher might need to work with the printer to get it, which might require committing to a certain minimum print run. That could significantly increase the cost of printing the book.

Length

While the length of the book is obviously dependent on the length of the written work, it is still a choice that must be made. As mentioned before, books are printed in signatures, or increments of pages. This allows the printer to print as many pages as possible on one huge sheet that is then folded and cut into the final book. Therefore, the total page count must be a multiple of the signature (usually 16).

The length also has a subconscious effect on the potential buyer. A book that is marketed as easy-to-read and manageable, better be on the shorter side. Similarly, more comprehensive books are expected to be longer.

Trim

Standard book trim sizes, produced and printed at traditional manufacturing and printing presses, achieve the greatest economies of scale, and are the most cost efficient. There are times when a title's content—especially for highly illustrated or gift titles—might require or suggest a unique trim size or binding. Costs associated with these unique sizes will have an impact on the overall cost of manufacturing the book.

Also, oversized or unusual trim size could force a title to be displayed outside of the category, or relegated to a top or bottom shelf with other unique trim sizes. Every effort should be made to have the titles displayed within appropriate categories. There is already enough competition; don't make consumers search for your book.

There are, however, times when the retail environment will dictate the trim size. If the title is going to be sold primarily through specialty stores—craft books come to mind—the only display opportunities might be in racks sized for magazines. Trim size decisions are often dictated by the merchandising opportunities.

Consult the printer about what their standard trim sizes are and what their capabilities are.

Format

The hardcover versus paperback choice largely depends on the book's genre and the author's status. If the author has developed a loyal following, and devoted readers want to be the first to read the next book, they might be willing to pay more for a hardcover format. Others will wait for the cheaper paperback or would prefer to read an ebook. Keepsakes are in hardcover; beach reading is paperback. Reference books are tomes; travel books shouldn't weigh down your backpack.

The two most important questions that need to be asked are: Where will the book achieve most of its sales? What format is appropriate for that channel?

If most of the book's sales will be through traditional book channels, then the publisher needs to consider the competitive marketplace. If the bookstore buyers are saying that this is a price-sensitive market and that trade paperback is the preferred format, then it seems the decision is pretty clear. If the bulk of the books are going to be sold at the author's speaking engagements or to libraries, then a hardcover might be appropriate.

If this is the author's first foray into self-publishing and the market for the book isn't clear yet, it will be much more economical to print a small digital print run of paperbacks and then reprint later if there turns out to be demand for the book. It is rarely economical to print fewer than a couple thousand hardcover books in one print run.

Cover Stock

A book cover or jacket is typically coated with a laminate to protect the design. (Almost any book in a bookstore will have this laminate coating.) The two primary options for that coating are glossy and matte. Which one is appropriate is dependent on the effect the book is trying to achieve, the book's genre, and that genre's trends. Business books are often glossy hardcovers, while literary novels are often matte. A simple walk around a local bookstore will help any author or publisher decide this matter. But if the publisher wants the book to stand out from the crowd with a fancier cover and higher production values, other options exist to help achieve that.

Spot gloss fancies up a matte cover by putting a glossy coating on portions of the design, often the title or a part of the cover image. Embossing is another option. This treatment raises parts of the design, giving the cover a three-dimensional feel. Often science fiction books and other mass-market paperbacks will emboss the title and the author name.

If the author has won awards or has some other honor that sets him or her apart from the crowd, adding a foil stamp is also an option. The cheapest method is to design something that looks like a stamp and print in metallic ink. The next option is to use real foil, and cut out the text so that the ink below the foil colors the words. The third option, and the most expensive, is to use foil and emboss the text and design on top of it.

When planning to use any of the additional cover printing options, be sure to allow extra funds in the book's budget and extra time at the printer. Usually printers will ask for an extra week or two when working with foil stamps and embossing.

Other Binding Considerations

When printing a hardcover, there are more decisions to be made in addition to the paper and cover stock. The first of these is the case. It is possible to print the jacket image directly onto the case as well, so that the book looks identical with or without its jacket. This is a popular option with children's books. Be aware that this adds to the overall costs, since more ink is used. Another option is to use cloth on the case, and emboss the title onto the spine with foil. The printer can offer samples of all the possible cloth colors and foils in order to make the choice.

Hardcovers also include endpapers, which are typically a blank single-color piece of paper that lies between the hardcover case and the first and last of the pages. Often the endpaper color is chosen to complement the color of the cloth or the jacket. Finally, tail ends must be chosen, which are the pieces of thread visible at the base of the spine in between the cover and the pages. These also come in a wide range of colors, so be sure to check with the printer for samples.

3

Production

Printer Selection

There are a number of key questions to consider when selecting a printer:

- Are they experienced book printers?
- What is their reputation in the publishing community?
- Can their staff and facility handle all of this book's special printing requirements (e.g. inserts, special trim, end papers)?
- Where are they located? Do they routinely ship to warehouses? What are their standard shipping costs?
- Do they have the ability to pack per specific warehouse or distributor instructions?
- Can they create and pack any special displays?
- What are their average turnaround times and minimums for reprints?

When considering printers, ask about recent printing jobs

for other publishers. While their own samples may give a sense of the quality of their work, it is worth the time to visit a local bookstore and consider how those titles appear at retail. Check the printing and binding. Is it up to the standards required for this project? Look at the fit and fold on hardcover jackets. Are they within acceptable standards? Are the trade paperback covers curling on the shelves? Are the boards warping?

Speak to the warehouse and customer service people. They are on the front lines of receiving and redistributing issues, and they can tell you if there are any special require-ments the printer should know about.

There are additional challenges when working with an international printer, such as additional time and costs for shipping and customs, and the time and minimums required for a cost-effective reprint. There are also freight-forwarding charges once the books reach the port of entry and have to go through customs. If overseas printing is new to the publisher, a reputable international printing broker can be an indispens-able partner in the process.

The first step of actually working with a printer is getting estimates. Sales associates will specify what information they need, but generally all of the specs (page count, trim size, hardcover vs. paperback, glossy vs. matte) are necessary. This is the time to explore the options, so request estimates for a few different paper options and the addition of a foil stamp or embossing. It is always worthwhile to ask for multiple print numbers to get a sense of where the price break points are.

Print Number

Selecting the best printer for every specific project is important, but deciding on the right quantity to print is critical. The
printer is likely to suggest printing more copies rather than
fewer because "The unit cost will be lower." The distributor
will return the favor by asking, "How many does the publisher
want to print?"

Deciding on just the right number is not an exact science. Each title is different and requires its own unique set of
calculations.

When deciding on the quantity of the first print run, there
are a few general rules to follow. First, be conservative. Books
can always be reprinted if there is sufficient demand, though
be sure that the printer can efficiently and dependably deliver
the reprints in a timely fashion. This is particularly important
during peak print times, especially during the late summer and
early fall.

Read the printing and binding agreement's fine print
regarding the over/under delivery of the requested print quantity. If the agreement has a 5% to 10% over/under clause
which allows a printer to deliver a quantity that is up to 5%
(or 10%) over or under the stated print quantity, make certain
that stock won't run out if the book is short-printed. Establish
a printing order that is "no less than…" so that a minimum
quantity that will cover advance orders but also sales rep
and account samples, publicity review copies, author special

orders, and other bulk purchases and reorders is guaranteed for delivery.

Second, if the book is aimed at the bookstore market, never print more than six months' anticipated supply. If re-printing a predictable backlist title, the publisher might want to print up to a year's worth of inventory, but remember, this is tying up cash.

Third, use the sales history of similar books to judge this book's needs. Ingram's ipage or Nielsen's BookScan, websites your distributor might be able to access, are great references resource.

Printing

Once the printer is selected, be sure to ask them for a cover template, as well as their requested format for interior files. Most printers differ slightly, so it is always advantageous to ask early on. Communicate this information to the designers as soon as possible. This will make the process of getting files to the printer much simpler down the road.

When the files are ready to send, the designer should send a zipped file complete with the source files (InDesign is most commonly used), as well as all links and fonts found in the design, and a high-resolution and low-resolution (or hi-res and lo-res) PDF version of the completed file. This should be sent to the printer in its entirety.

Once the pre-press process is started on the printer's end,

they will send the publisher proofs of the cover and the interior. This is also specific to the printer. Some prefer to work with "soft" (aka digital) proofs, while others will always send a hard copy. Soft proofs are generally enough for simple black and white paperbacks, but more complicated books with inserts or images may require a hard proof. It is always recommended to see a hard proof of the cover. This stage is mostly to check for color and alignment, and to ensure that all the pages appear in the correct order. Once the proofs have been double and triple checked, the print run will commence.

Cartoning

The printer should put the books into cartons (cardboard boxes) in preparation for shipping. Check with the warehouse for their carton and labeling guidelines. Books should be placed flat in the carton and not on the spine or page edges. Most of the carriers such as UPS will not be as careful with your cartons as the publisher or author is, so the corrugated cardboard used in the carton should be strong enough to withstand shipping the carton of books across the country several times. Strength of cardboard is measured in a few different ways, but "275 pound" corrugated should be sufficient. (This means that the cardboard can withstand pressure up to 275 pounds per square inch.)

The warehouse may also have requirements or preferences regarding the packing material (also called dunnage). The packing material prevents the books from sliding around in the carton and thus reduces damage. Styrofoam peanuts can be messy, so they may not be allowed. Other types of dunnage include cardboard, bubble wrap, paper, or air packs. If the books are stacked into two columns, side by side, a piece of cardboard should be between the columns so that the books do not rub against each other. If the book is a traditional size (5 x 8 or 6 x 9), the printer will probably have appropriate cartons, so dunnage will not be needed on the sides. However, packing material may be needed at the top of the carton.

The carton count is an important number. This is simply the number of books in a carton. The printer should not put 25 books in some cartons and 30 in another. (If they do this, they are not a very professional printer.) Many accounts order in full cartons, so it is important that everyone is aware of this number and the distributor knows if the carton quantity changes after a new print run.

The cartons should be clearly labeled so that everyone knows the contents. The carton label should at least include the following information: title of the book, ISBN, publisher name, and quantity of books in the carton. Some printers also include the carton weight, their own name, and the date of the printing. The printer may be able to include this information in barcoded format. Again, check with the warehouse to determine their requirements.

Shipping

Almost every warehouse has specific picking, packing, and receiving requirements that should be shared with the printer as early as possible. Most printers can handle these directions with little or no supervision. However, if the printer is not familiar with book printing or a non-traditional package or format is being used, close attention must be paid to delivering the titles in a receivable condition. If the printer does not follow the warehouse's specific instructions, the publisher is likely to incur extra charges and experience delays.

Once books are received in the warehouse they will be picked and packed to meet account specifications. All chain retailers have specifications with regard to the boxes that books are packed in. For example, Barnes & Noble requires that each carton be printed with the title, ISBN, quantity in the box, bar code, etc. If books are shipping directly from the printer to an account (sometimes called drop shipping), the sales people or distributor should advise the publisher on this key area and the publisher in turn will need to advise the printer.

Work with the salespeople to identify any account-specific picking and packing instructions that are beyond the standard requirements. This could include promotional displays, clip strips, or other merchandising items. If they have the capabilities, it may be more economical for the printer to pack to these requirements to allow for direct shipment to the accounts or quick delivery and turnaround at the warehouse.

Confirm and schedule all warehouse delivery dates. A visit to the distributor's warehouse will give the author and publisher a keen appreciation of the nuances of handling thousands of titles being shipped to thousands of locations each day. The more seamless the procedure, the easier it will be to meet the book's target publication date.

There are times when things go wrong in the printing and binding process. Communicate any delays and changes, with anticipated new dates, to the sales team and warehouse staff as quickly as possible. This is particularly important if the title is scheduled for in-store promotions. If the books have not been received in time to be staged for the displays, the books may not get into the promotion.

Reprints

Congratulations! The book is selling and it is time for a reprint. Reprints are not an automatic process and the publisher needs to be aware of a number of things when planning a reprint.

Sometimes publishers are offered deals by their printer to print with an upgrade to the paper stock. The better stock is most likely excess special stock the printer used for another printing job. Sometimes, this can be a very attractive offer and the publisher can get a great deal. However, when it comes time to reprint the title, the original paper may no longer be in stock or available. Publishers are then challenged to decide either to order and purchase the original stock at a much higher price and perhaps experience a reprint delay, or have to change the paper to an inferior grade to keep costs under control. Changing paper grades can create issues with stock color compatibility with the cover and binding. Both printings can end up side-by-side on a bookshelf, and the differences often stand out even to the untrained eye. And, in some worst-case scenarios, the jackets might have to be redesigned to accommodate a larger or smaller spine, creating additional costs that will eat into profits.

Make certain that any corrections or changes are prepared and submitted in a timely fashion for every reprint. If prices are changing, make sure the ISBN and EAN codes reflect the change. No one wants to lose profits at point-of-sale or spend money to sticker incorrect prices if the codes aren't updated.

Ebooks

Ebooks have quickly become a common format in the publishing industry, so it is absolutely necessary to plan for and create an ebook alongside the physical paperback or hardcover. A common concern is that ebooks might cannibalize physical sales. The truth of the matter is that physical book sales are shrinking whether ebooks are published or not. The Institute for Publishing Research projects that the physical book market will decrease by 2% over the next five years while the ebook market will continue to grow. The good news is that by making titles available as ebooks, they become accessible to new groups of readers. The more places and greater ease with which people can buy the book—in stores and online—the more opportunities there are to make a sale.

■ **Formats.** As with physical books, ebooks have different formats. There are two major types: reflowable and fixed layout. The most common reflowable vendor is EPUB. Reflowable ebooks have some unique characteristics that are beneficial, but sometimes difficult to deal with. A reflowable ebook allows readers to control aspects of the book such as the font size and typeface on their reading device. This can be useful to a reader who requires large print, but it is a nightmare for a book designer. When a physical book layout is created, words, text boxes, and pictures are placed purposely on the page to create an easy-to-read design. But in reflowable ebooks, the reader can change the font or page size, and the entire layout changes. When designing the book, consider how it will look in a reflowable format. As ebooks grow in popularity, more ebooks may be sold than physical books, so both should be equally appealing. EPUB is best for simple text-based books but does not work well with highly designed titles or poetry.

    With the fixed layout format, what the reader sees is controlled because the reader cannot manipulate the format in any way. One popular version of fixed layout is a

PDF. The final file sent to the printer is basically an ebook, but with a few important changes: decreasing the overall size of the file and linking the table of contents. Often this reworked PDF is referred to as a "web PDF." This format is not nearly as popular or common as the reflowable format, but some libraries will request it, and certain readers prefer it.

Additional fixed layout formats are becoming more popular, such as the fixed layout EPUB. Fixed layout EPUBs are fully-functional HTML-based ebook files in every way; however, the specific styles and layouts used in these files are not reflowable like standard EPUB files. Most of the major retailers support some form of a fixed layout, but this type of ebook is still new and is very expensive to create.

- *Broad Access.* When distributing an ebook, publishers should target as many channels and retailers as possible. A few companies, such as Amazon, Apple, and Barnes & Noble, have a large share of the ebook market, but it is important not to ignore readers on other platforms. A good distributor will reach all platforms, including libraries. An author's biggest fans may shop at Kobo and they shouldn't miss out on reading the book.

- *Price Promotion.* One of the best things about ebooks is price flexibility. Because ebooks do not have any paper or printing costs, and there is no price printed on the back of the book, publishers can change the price as often as they want. This allows the publisher to use price as a tactical tool to sell books instead of a static choice made when they printed the book.

The most obvious and common tactic is to lower the ebook price for a select amount of time through certain vendors. A low price reduces the cost of entry for a new reader and should increase sales if promoted effectively. A price promotion can last any length of time, but between one week and one month is usually ideal. One or two days are not enough time for people to find the book and let their friends know about the great deal. Over a month and the publisher might be losing money to people who are willing to buy the book at full price.

A particularly useful way to use a price promotion is in conjunction with some other marketing or publicity. For example, if the author is being interviewed by a publication, he might mention that his book will be available at a discounted price for the following week. This could convince more readers to buy the book quickly, which increases the title's popularity and moves it up in internet searches. This makes it easier for the next potential readers to locate.

■ *Piracy.* Piracy is a concern whenever intellectual property, like music, an ebook, or even a physical book, is disseminated. The music industry found that piracy develops in response to an unmet market demand.

The best way to prevent piracy of titles is by making them legally available in digital format. In addition, the digital marketplace has developed ways to mitigate the risk of piracy. Retailers apply digital rights management (DRM) technology to the books they sell to limit piracy.

Marketing Uses

One of the benefits of an ebook is that once it is created, there is no cost to create additional copies. This means that an ebook can be an inexpensive way to market the title. For example, the ebook can be used as an inexpensive galley or advanced reading copy, or the ebook can be emailed to people who might consider reviewing it.

4

Sales and Distribution

::

After creating a book, it is necessary to find a way to sell it. The book-selling landscape is complicated, and requires an expert with established relationships to convince bookstores, wholesalers, and online retailers to take a chance on the book and buy copies. A good distributor can take care of all of those details along with many others. Distributors tend to take a percentage of net sales in exchange for these services. Then again, not every book is meant to be sold into the book trade.

Options

■ *Direct local sale.* If the book will only be sold to the author's personal community, in the back of the room at speaking engagements, or at conventions, then selling the book directly may be the best option. Keep in mind that many successful publishing programs start out from direct local sales. At some point it will become necessary to transition to a full scale distribution model in order to take sales to the next level. While direct sales can be more profitable on a micro scale, the sales will eventually plateau, and growth to an expanded national market will be unlikely.

- *Online retailers.* Online retailers include accounts such as Amazon.com, BN.com, and Overstock.com. Virtually every retailer (including Walmart and Target) now has a presence on the internet. A good distributor will have a direct relationship with many of these accounts as well as relationships with the wholesalers that service them. A distributor will help to coordinate inventory availability for direct purchasing as well as inventory management at the wholesalers in order to maintain stock availability. Accurate data importing is critical in order to have accurate listings online, including correct covers and book descriptions. The sales manager should be looking for marketing opportunities with these accounts as well.

  If the book doesn't have a distributor, it is still possible to make it available on Amazon.com, either through their CreateSpace program or by creating a relationship with them as a seller. More information about that is available on the Amazon website.

- *Distributor.* Book distributors represent the interests and activities of book publishers. A good distributor will allow even the smallest publisher to play on a level playing field with the largest publishing houses, providing them full access to key buyers, data systems, and marketing programs. There are two primary functions of a book distributor: sales and distribution.

Because of the explosive growth of the independent publishing community within the trade publishing industry, the role of distributors has become ever more crucial. There are several reasons for this: first, key wholesalers have decided to stop working directly with smaller independent publishers. Second, chain retailers insist that independent publishers use third party distributors as the way into their stores. And third, distributors have become very professional in providing important selling and fulfillment services to client publishers. Retail and wholesale accounts require sophisticated data entry processes as well as EDI ordering and shipping requirements. A qualified distributor is set up to handle these requirements and will stay on top of the changes that frequently occur.

Selling Landscape

■ *National Superstores.* The landscape for national bookstore chains has changed dramatically over the past few years. Many of the mall-based stores, such as Waldenbooks and B. Dalton, are gone. Borders has also closed, leaving Barnes and Noble as the only major national bookstore chain in the United States, with slightly over 700 stores. It is also worth noting that with the expansion of online book sales and the growth of ebooks, brick and mortar stores have reduced the area available for book merchandise, and bookstores are expanding into non-book product lines such as games, educational materials, puzzles, and stationery. B&N has dedicated the front of their store (what used to be prime space for promoting books) to their Nook ebook program and accessories. With the growth of online book sales, bookstores are no longer carrying a deep backlist of books on physical shelves. They carry the top-selling books and provide internet access for special orders, even at computer kiosks located in the store. While this development presents a challenge for publishers, an experienced sales management team can help navigate through the possibilities to achieve optimum distribution with the right books at the right place at the right time. A sales manager will also be in communication with the marketing departments for these chains, nominating appropriate titles for placement in store displays. Publishers are required to pay for special in-store placement, such as seasonal table-top displays.

- *National Wholesalers.* People often confuse book wholesalers and book distributors. Both are essential to a publisher's success, if not survival, but they differ greatly in the services they provide.

The book wholesaler should be seen as a service provider to bookstores, internet retailers, libraries, and other markets. They do not create demand; rather, they efficiently respond to demand, whatever the cause and whatever the title. They envision their task as serving the interests of bookstores and similar outlets. Their main objective is to get Product A to Store B in the shortest possible time and at the lowest possible cost. Two of the largest are Ingram and Baker & Taylor. Wholesalers are a resource for a wide base of customers. A sales management team will need to work closely with them to monitor stock levels, review postings and bibliographic data, and participate in marketing programs that reach out to their customer base. An effective sales and distribution team will leverage the book's distribution position with wholesalers in order to reach an extremely wide market, one that would not be cost effective to reach any other way.

Internet Retailers. Two major internet booksellers are Amazon.com and Barnesandnoble.com, but there are many others. Most other major accounts, independent bookstores, and specialty retailers also maintain an online presence. The beauty of the Internet market is the speed and acceptance with which the books will be featured online. There are no "key buyers" per se who decide whether a book will be bought. Rather, there are "editors" whose main task is to ensure that all data pertaining to a book is featured on their web pages.

When a consumer is drawn to a book through a review, word-of-mouth, promotion, or browsing and they click to buy the book, it can theoretically be shipped within twenty-four hours. Both of the above internet booksellers have warehouses across the country and will generally stock a minimum quantity of every title. Internet retailers also use national and regional wholesalers as back up. Wholesalers will ship directly to consumers on behalf of the internet retailer.

It is important for the author to monitor his own on-line presence with these accounts. Make certain that the final covers are posted and any price or other information-al updates have been made. Offer as much information online as possible to help sell the features and benefits of the author's titles

■ **Regional Chains.** Regional chains, such as Books-A-Million and Hastings, continue to do well in the markets they have established over the years. While Books-A-Million has been operating primarily in the south, they have recently expanded through the acquisition of more than 30 Borders locations in other parts of the country. Hastings stores are located primarily in Texas and the southwest and thrive in smaller markets where there are no superstores. Both accounts as well as other smaller chains were early adopters into the non-book market, supplementing shrinking book sales by selling greeting cards, plush toys, collectibles, and educational materials. These accounts maintain category buyers, and they need to be sold well in advance of publication date. They are very selective and have specific guidelines that need to be followed in order to be considered for placement in stores. There are marketing opportunities with these accounts as well. Regional chains will order from distributors directly as well as through wholesalers.

■ *Independent Bookstores.* While many independent stores have closed over the years, there has been a resurgence of the savvy independent bookstores that provide superior customer service and develop customer loyalty through personal connections and in-store activities. Many independents will focus on a specific category of books, such as mysteries or children's books.

There are many excellent independents such as The Tattered Cover in Denver, Malaprop's in Asheville, and Powell's in Portland which have grown stronger with the increased competition. The independent bookstores can be proud that they "discover" writers and often help make a book a bestseller by talking to each other and their loyal customer base. Classic word-of-mouth marketing often produces a groundswell that helps push a title onto a bestseller list. Independent bookstores in the author's local area are worth targeting, especially because book-signing events will guarantee that a certain amount of books will be purchased by the store. Many independents use online catalog services such as Edelweiss to assist with their ordering. An effective sales approach would also include targeted telesales activities, robust listings with wholesalers, in-store events where the author is well known, social networking, and email blasts, complete with ordering instructions.

■ ***Wholesale Clubs.*** Wholesale clubs include accounts such as Costco and Sam's Club. While placement in these accounts can be exciting, there is a great deal of risk involved. They require a substantial commitment of inventory, there is a steep discount involved, and the window for sales performance is small. If a title does not meet specific unit sales targets, the entire inventory and any backup inventory will be returned. It is important to work very closely with the sales team on placement opportunities for these accounts. Wherever possible, opt for a test in specific markets before launching nationally. A successful test will provide some level of confidence for a successful sell-through with a national roll out. The publisher will also need to consider how placement with these accounts will affect the book's position with other retailers. Whole-sale clubs will discount heavily, and sales may decline at other retail locations, where the publisher is receiving a better margin on the sale.

■ *Mass Merchandisers.* Walmart and Target are the largest mass merchandisers. They are very selective in their buying decisions, focusing on bestsellers, lead categories, and seasonal titles. If the book works in these outlets, it could mean sales of thousands of units. Many require minimum weekly per-store sales rates to keep titles at retail. If titles don't achieve these thresholds, they will be pulled from the shelves, often resulting in disappointing sales and high return rates. Keep in mind that mass merchandisers are not always looking to stock titles that would appeal to the same customer who shops in a traditional bookstore. They do not carry a deep selection. Strong categories include romance, bestselling fiction, children's and young adult, cooking, and pop culture.

Everyone would like to see appropriate titles accepted by mass merchandisers, and it can be accomplished with a sales team that has the right contacts with buyers and also with the wholesalers that work with these accounts. It is important to work closely with the sales team, discussing the viability of different titles and the potential for the books to sell through at these outlets. Proceed with caution, because a big up-front buy can require a larger print quantity, and it can sometimes mean substantial returns and much-reduced profitability.

■ *Supermarkets and Drug Stores.* Supermarket chains, such as Safeway and Kroger, and drugstore chains, such as Rite

Aid and CVS, work closely with regional distributors to determine what books to carry. Sales are limited and returns can be high. There is also a risk for the return of damaged books from these locations. With that said, the right book in the right market can sell very well. Some chains have developed health and wellness sections in their stores, in addition to the typical mass market paperback, children's, and magazine categories. The sales team will need to work closely with the local and national distributors in order to work effectively with these accounts. If an author has a strong constituency in a particular market and a book that is appropriate, it is possible to contact a local supermarket, and if the store decides to bring in the book, they will contact its distributor.

■ *College Bookstores*. College bookstores include stores operated by B&N College as well as Follett (an education-oriented wholesaler). There are also college bookstores that are run independently. The sales team should work with buyers at the national level (B&N, Follett, and National Association of College Stores) as well as with national wholesalers to make sure that titles are presented. Accounts such as National Association of College Stores (NACS) do have topical catalogs where titles can be highlighted. There is a cost for this service.

■ *Regional Wholesalers.* Regional wholesalers help to fill in the gaps and offer coverage for special markets, such as health food chains, wellness centers, outdoor recreation chains, etc. Many of these wholesalers, such as Bookazine, will ship for Amazon and B&N as well as for local retailers in their markets. It is important to keep these accounts up-to-date on all new titles. They are a necessary part of the overall sales picture.

▨ *Library Wholesalers.* The library market is a significant market for both Ingram and Baker & Taylor. Others include Brodart, Bookazine, and Blackwell North America. It is important for the sales group to work with wholesalers to ensure that the data submitted to libraries is correct and timely. Everything from BISAC codes to Library of Congress numbers is supplied to the wholesalers by the sales team.

Public libraries represent the largest segment of the library market. School libraries generally refer to kindergarten through high school, and book buying is vetted stringently to make sure that books are age-appropriate. Academic libraries are found on all college campuses and research institutes, and they generally buy only serious research works, books written by their faculty, or titles requested by faculty members.

Public library acquisition librarians make their purchases based on reviews appearing in publications like *Publishers Weekly, Library Journal, Kirkus Reviews*, and

The American Library Association (ALA) *Booklist*. Many libraries compile category-specific suggested reading lists based upon reviews and their own circulation information. These lists are helpful when identifying a book's competition.

■ *Book Clubs.* Direct Brands, Inc. with its affiliate Bookspan, operates over twenty-four different direct-to-consumer club brands, including Book of the Month Club, History Book Club, and Crossings. Books can be presented for nomination. They are very selective, and titles must fit in the proper club category. Publishers are competing against proven authors with a track record of sales. Expect to sell in at a very deep discount if a title is accepted. Book clubs might also license the right to print the book and print it themselves in exchange for an advance and royalties.

■ *Consignment Wholesalers.* Consignment wholesalers, which include accounts such as Gazelle for international sales and Quality and Unique for library sales, effectively sell to their markets and offer quick order turnaround, as well as specific requirements for the customers, such as proper reference coding for libraries. The consignment model is somewhat different from the typical wholesaler model where the wholesaler purchases books up front. With a consignment arrangement, a limited amount of inventory is consigned with the wholesaler and a purchase is made once they ship the book to their customer. The distributor needs to maintain proper records for the allocation of this consigned inventory and the recording of sales.

Special Sales

Special sales and distribution involve selling books to non-traditional book retailers and wholesalers. These special markets are comprised of a wide variety of retail, wholesale, and premium companies. Special sales outlets include warehouse clubs, airport stores, supermarkets, department stores, drug stores, gift shops, home-shopping networks, online retailers, museums, zoos, parks, and many others. It also includes selling to wholesalers that are typically category-driven and service-specific specialty stores which exclusively distribute to these retailers. Many of these retailers and wholesalers have specific niches that they cater to, like kitchen stores that carry cookbooks, for example, or hotel stores that carry travel guidebooks. Books can sometimes be secondary in these markets, and become tie-ins to specific themes or events, like a barbecue cookbook in the grilling section of a housewares store. Special sales require a great deal of research, outreach, and follow up in order to make a sale, and often it is necessary to have a relationship with the right contacts. For this reason, going through a distributor is more efficient.

Premiums and incentives comprise another segment of

special sales. This involves selling to corporations, government agencies, non-profits, etc. This would be for books used as premiums, gifts, or incentives. These companies use books as motivational tools for their employees, as gifts for their customers, as premiums to lure new customers, or as a thank-you gift at the end of a cruise vacation. Associations, schools, and military bases could also fall into this category. This category also requires a great deal of work to make the sale, but a premium sale can be very lucrative.

Interacting with a Distributor

If working with a distributor, the author still has a role in the selling process. The distributor can only make a sale if all the necessary information has been provided, including data and marketing details. The sales reps will do their best to become familiar with every book, but it's impossible for them to read every one. Therefore, the publisher has to provide them with ammunition in the sales meeting. With this help, they will do the best possible job for every client.

Different distributors work with their client publishers differently. For Midpoint, the tip sheet or sales sheet needs to be completed at least six months prior to the publication date. The tip sheet includes the cover image, title, ISBN, author name and biography, all relevant specs including BISAC codes, a short description, and sales points. The short description is more compact than the back cover copy, although they are often similar. The main difference is that the sell sheet description is targeted to the professionals of the book industry rather than consumers. Sales points are the details that set the book apart from others. Some might include the author's credentials or past bestsellers, if the author is working with a publicist, or any scheduled media appearances.

As often as possible, it is best to get samples, presskits, and other promotional items to the sales reps so they can pass them along to their buyers. This is particularly important at the larger accounts where there are many buyers. Make sure certain materials are delivered to the right people in a timely fashion to impact an order.

5

Marketing and PR

arketing is a very misunderstood word when it comes to selling books through bookstores. With most consumer brands, marketing is based on sophisticated and expensive testing. Almost nothing is left to chance, which is not so much a guarantee of success as it is a reduction of the risk of failure. On the other hand, book launches involve little or no testing. It might be compared to a baseball batter taking a swing at a curve ball. If he gets a hit one-third of the time, he is considered a star. The same is true for many trade books on a publisher's list. A few home runs pay for the missed swings. Larger publishers try to mitigate this risk by finding well-known authors who have previous successes, or barring that, they use the media as extensively as possible to create buzz and sales. But if a publisher is publishing just one book, it's critical to make every effort count—there's only one shot at hitting a home run.

The primary objective of a marketing campaign is to deliver sales at a profit. It is imperative to make the most of the publisher's money and focus marketing and publicity efforts on the demographic that can most relate to the title. No book is for everyone—everyone does not need your book. Focus on the title's core audience and find the largest group of people who may be interested enough to explore the title further and ultimately buy it. The four most important questions to consider when planning the title's marketing are variations on the questions the sales rep asks the editor or publisher, the book buyer asks the sales rep, and the TV producer asks the publicist.

- Who is the target audience for this book?
- How will that consumer find out about this book?
- How is this book different from every other title on the shelf?
- Who is the author, and why should the consumer pay attention to what the author has to say?

The answers to these questions should be part of the initial publishing decision process. The discussion begins in earnest and a marketing plan begins to take shape the moment the contract is signed.

The successful plan first identifies the target audience, their demographics and interests. Where do they get their information? What newspapers and magazines are they most likely to read? What radio or television shows are they most likely to watch? What web sites do they visit? Are there associations or professional organizations catering to the market? Are courses being taught? Where do these potential readers shop, what formats do they prefer, and how much are they willing to spend?

To market the book successfully, a clear, consistent, and compelling message must be presented to engage every potential consumer to consider buying the book. Make sure everyone within the publishing organization understands the strategy. Encourage them to communicate this message in images and text, supporting every sales and marketing activity in the most cost-efficient manner. Everyone needs to be on the same page.

Timeline for Marketing and PR

Ideally, marketing begins when the publisher decides to publish a book. Too often, marketing is left to the last minute, but successful marketing is a long-term proposition. A plan should be created immediately, and it should be constantly reviewed and refined throughout the publishing process.

Here is an approximate marketing timeline. The budget and expectations for the book might change if and when some of these steps are completed.

Immediately:

- Decide on a title, format, and other specs.
- Begin working on a cover.
- Figure out if there are any major conferences, holidays, or other relevant or notable events around the publication date that can be leveraged to help promote the book. Also, pay attention to whether there are any major events that might make it hard to get publicity or attention for the book.
- If there is already a mailing list, start getting it in order and building it so it can be used when the book is ready. If there isn't one yet, start one! It's not too late to begin building a following.
- Build a website for the book and consider beginning a blog.

Once the manuscript is finished:

- Send it to other authors and prominent authorities in the same field to get advance endorsement quotes.
- Set a budget for the promotion and make a plan that takes into account how much there is to spend and where the budget should be focused.

6-9 months in advance of publication:

- Begin talking to publicists if hiring one is an option.
- Print advance reading copies (ARCs) and distribute them to long-lead magazines and publications, and the sales team.

- Make decisions about whether or not to run advertisements, and start gathering information on pricing, design specifications, and deadlines.

3-6 months in advance:

- Work on setting up events at bookstores and other organizations.
- Decide on a publicist and the length of the campaign.
- Send advance copies to trade review publications (most require at least 3-4 months' lead time).
- Ads are probably due around now, depending on what types of ads are being placed.

1-3 months in advance:

- Begin promoting the book and any events around its launch to the author's network.
- Reach out to bloggers and online publications.
- Update the website; ramp up blogging activities.

Pub date:

- Consider launching with a specific event or promotional push, even if it's a virtual one.
- Push the book hard to the author's networks and the networks of organizations that have gotten behind the book's message.
- Try to schedule some big media around the publication day so the author can start to create sales. Block out a

few weeks around publication, especially the week of
publication, and make sure the author is available for any
media opportunities that come along.

First 3 months:

- Keep doing events and promoting them to the author's
  network.
- Try to keep pushing interesting angles to the media, or
  figure out ways that the book is relevant to what is being
  covered by the media at any given time.

4 months after publication:

- Evaluate the book's promotional strategy, figure out what
  has been most successful and what has failed or not given
  the results expected.
- Take stock of whether there is money left in the budget.
  If the book is selling well, consider establishing a new
  budget to keep the momentum going or increase the rate
  of sales. If the book has not sold well, weigh carefully
  whether it is worth committing any additional money to
  the project.
- Come up with a new strategy for how to keep promoting
  the book.
- If the book originally launched in hardcover or ebook-only
  formats, consider whether publishing a paperback might
  help gain new sales. Begin planning the paperback at
  least 9-12 months before its publication date.

Publicity

Publicity will make or break any book. First, the book's angle has to be established. Maybe it's a mother/daughter story perfect for Mother's Day, or a book of love letters perfect for Valentine's Day, or the perfect YA sci-fi book for all those teens who have nothing to read after finishing *Twilight*. Once the niche market is established, everything written, said, or presented should have that persuasive angle. When deciding on this angle, research comparable titles and consider what makes this book different or better than the successful ones.

Next, the keys to publicity are persuasion, persistence, and patience. After the angle is established and the press release and pitch letter are created, all material should be reviewed. How does it sound? Is it convincing? Is it short and sweet? Does it stay on point? (Note: Stay away from empty adjectives, i.e. unique, one-of-a-kind, wonderful, excellent, etc. Use concrete ones: easy-to-read, inviting, humorous, entertaining, enlightening, etc.)

The next step is to make the pitch. What is pitching exactly? It is focused outreach designed to interest someone in your book or author. Pitching can be done in many ways—phone calls, emails, letters in the mail, mailing out the advance reading copy with a letter and press release, and even via social media, such as LinkedIn, Facebook, Twitter, and Google+.

When pitching, the appropriate lead time must be taken into account, which is how far in advance the publication finalizes their editorial content before publication. In order to be featured in glossy magazines, pitch four to six months in advance. Weekly newspapers require four to six weeks, and daily newspapers require one to three weeks. Radio talk shows require one week to one month. Bloggers are more flexible, but seven to ten days is a general guideline. If pitching a review rather than an article, more time must be allowed. Industry review publications like *Publisher's Weekly, Kirkus Reviews, Bookpage, Booklist*, and *Library Journal* require galleys four months prior to pub date.

The varied lead times require a great deal of planning and organization far in advance. If there are plans to tie the book into Valentine's Day, pitching articles for magazines should begin in July or August, and for blogs in January.

When sending pitches, it is helpful to find out how each media outlet and contact person prefers to be reached. It seems that now, most prefer email. When emailing them, write a catchy subject, copy-and-paste the pitch letter and press release in the body, and make a link to the book's retailer page or website. To find contact information, there are online directories, such as Agility, Vocus, and Cision, that will list names and direct contact information, as well as subjects of interest and preferred contact method. These databases can be accessed for a fee. Cision also publishes Bacon's Media Directory, which is filled with all the relevant up-to-date information. If this is too expensive, media professionals can be found through their individual websites. Another option is to use a mass-mailing service such as Constant Contact, which will not only send the email, but also track the status of the pitches.

Above everything else, the most important key is persistence. Expect that 5–10% of pitches will get a hit, or a reply. Once the media's interest is piqued, make sure to inquire when they will publish the review, or begin discussions on the author's interview availability. For the others who don't respond, it will be time to follow up two to three weeks later.

To follow up, create a new email subject line and opening line or two for the pitch. If there is no initial response or interest, the physical book can be sent along with the pitch and press release to the top media outlets. Also, write a two-minute phone pitch and begin calling them. The main goal is to speak with the intention of creating a relationship.

Once this is all done, it comes down to patience; however, the job of getting publicity is never done. While you wait for responses, create a different angle to reach a new target audience. Sometimes it takes media professionals weeks and even months to sort through emails, so out-of-the-blue responses are totally possible.

Above all else, pitching the book and the author comes down to professionalism. The writing represents the product, so be mindful of grammar, punctuation, and spelling. Never trust spell check—homophones (their, they're, there) are never detected. Research templates for this type of writing so that what is delivered is up to the industry's standards. Publicity is all about the public—is the writing good enough for the world to see? It should be.

If this all seems overwhelming, there are many great freelance publicists and publicity firms that will work with authors on a project basis. Frequently, even authors that are published by major houses will take a portion of their advances and hire an independent publicist to ensure that they get the attention for their book that they desire. Many independent publicists have strong relationships with the media already in place, which can help authors get more attention for their books than they can hope to get on their own. Some publicists specialize in a specific area such as cookbooks, parenting, memoirs, or fiction. Authors should make sure to ask publicists they are considering about what areas the publicist focuses on and where they have gotten hits for their clients in the past. A publicist should be able to show prospective clients the results of previous successful campaigns and put them in touch with references.

To find the right publicist, authors should ask people they are working with for references, or check MediaBistro.com and other online publishing resources. Book Expo America is also a good place to meet publicists. Some PR firms keep blogs that describe the process and offer tips to authors. It is best to talk to a few different publicists to get a sense of what they can offer, what they charge, and whether they are a good fit for the project. The right publicist can be invaluable to the successful promotion of a book.

Book Signings and Events

Years ago, publishers considered most bookstore-related events to be a waste of time, particularly if the author was not a major celebrity. Times have changed. Today, most bookstores encourage events and even employ event coordinators. These events can sometimes be extremely successful. However, there are a few rules to follow in order to save the author the embarrassment of having no one attend.

First, work very closely with the store owner or event coordinator. Find out what works for them and follow their advice. Second, if the event is in the author's hometown, make sure to invite people the author knows. Send out written invitations with a personal note. Third, if the author is away from home, try to schedule the event after the author appears on television or radio so the publicity can promote the event. Fourth, make sure books get to the event location on time and, just in case, the author should have a supply on hand. Finally, encourage the store to promote the book in-store at least a week before the appearance. This is grassroots marketing, and when handled professionally, it can help build recognition and sales. It's also helpful if a store reaches out to its mailing list and via social media to let local readers know about the event.

Make sure to follow up with the store after an event. Event coordinators and staff can give an honest appraisal of the appearance and offer suggestions for improvement.

Galleys, E-galleys, NetGalley

Review copies are the cornerstones of any publicity campaign. How many copies should be sent out? How many copies are in the budget? With the significant rise in readers and reviewers who are willing to review e-galleys, this does not have to break the bank. Typically, copies should go to the sales reps, who will present them to their buyers; to advance reviewers and long-lead publications; sometimes to potential endorsers who want to see a more finished product.

Many bookstores and libraries make their purchasing decisions based upon pre-publication reviews of bound pages or galleys in *Publishers Weekly, Library Journal, Kirkus Reviews*, and *Booklist*. Most of these publications require galleys three to four months before publication.

If the author wants to send samples to friends and family, it might make sense to wait for a finished book, which is usually cheaper than an advance reading copy. Advance reading copies might also be used for promotion at conferences and events (such as Book Expo America), foreign rights sales, and mailings to booksellers or librarians.

Internet Presence

It is critical for information about a book and its author to be available and easily discoverable on the internet. It is best if there is a site dedicated to a specific author or book. There are many free and inexpensive hosting sites, and free tools an author can use to create a basic page. However, much like the book cover, a website is an author's face online. For this reason, it can be a really useful investment to hire a professional web designer to create an attractive, easy-to-use site.

Publishers should search for their authors' names and book titles online to see what comes up. If none of the hits on the first page relate to the book or the author, readers won't be able to find the book even if they are looking for it. If there is a site for the book or the author but it does not appear on the first page of search results, the site's content might need to be optimized for search engines. There is a lot of information about search engine optimization (SEO) available, and many experts who can help make sure a site is optimized, which will increase the likelihood that it will be found through internet searches.

If the author or title already has a dedicated website, it is important to make sure that all the information on it is correct, and that it is appealing, informative, and easily navigable. If there is a blog on the site, make sure the author is posting to it regularly. Nothing disappoints readers more than discovering that the most recent entry in a blog is from several years ago. A well-written, interesting blog can be a great marketing tool for a book and help attract new readers.

It is also critical to make sure the information about the book is very visible. Ideally, there would be an image of the book cover on the front page (or every page) of the site, along with links or information about how to purchase it. The site should also include links to an author's social media pages, and allow fans to sign up for a mailing list if the author maintains one.

Social Networking

There have never been so many inexpensive and free tools for reaching out to potential readers as there are today. Many authors have achieved great results without spending any money by leveraging the power of social networking sites. However, it is important for authors to decide which sites to use and what they hope to achieve from them before diving into the world of social media.

Some social media options for a new title or author are to create author and book profiles on outlets such as Facebook, Twitter, and LinkedIn. Other popular sites include Goodreads, LibraryThing, Pinterest, Flickr, and Spotify, and many more are surely on the horizon. Authors who want to pursue a social networking strategy for promoting their books should always keep an eye on new developments online and consider ways they can use new tools to reach out to potential and current readers.

At this time, Facebook is the most established site and therefore the most necessary to help create visibility. Authors can make official "Book" and "Author" pages, which can include information about the book and author, pictures, polls, and more.

The author page should focus on the author, the book, and the author's expertise and interests. The book page can then focus more on coverage of the book, news, events, and other book-related information. Authors can use the book page to attempt to attract new fans by posting interesting and related stories, sample chapters, and parallels to other popular and successful books.

Social media is oriented toward making new contacts, so authors should "Friend" or "Follow" all of the people, markets, media, and other books they would like to reach. Then, authors can "Reply," "Retweet," or "Mention" these other profiles in order to get on their radar and hopefully form a coalition.

The other main goal of social media is to stay in touch with and develop relationships with the contacts one already has. For this reason the most important aspects of all social networking are frequency and consistency. Authors should brand all of their profiles similarly and keep the information on all the pages accurate.

It is also important to keep up with these sites, posting both Facebook updates and Tweets multiple times a day. Nothing is more of a deterrent than an abandoned page. Luckily, there are a number of social media dashboards, like Hootsuite, that make it possible for authors to stay visible on these sites without committing all their time to social media. These tools allow people to post on all of the sites at once, as well as schedule posts ahead of time so that they don't have to be attached to the computer all day long.

If this seems overwhelming or an impossibility, there are other options. More and more companies are popping up that offer social media design and maintenance services. Some of these are exceptional and can also design applications for an author's Facebook page that are specially created to draw new visitors and "Fans." Authors can also find a social media expert who will create their pages and keep them up-do-date.

Types of Advertising

◼ *Trade Advertising.* There are a number of publications catering to the book publishing and book selling business which are referred to as "book trade publications." Who reads the trade publications? Producers, authors, agents, foreign publishers, reviewers, the entire rights community, librarians, and, yes, the bookstore buyers.

There are a number of options to consider. Review the editorial calendars and see if there are specific issues that might be more beneficial to the publishing program. If working with a book distributor, the publisher may want to participate in their programs. But no matter what methods are chosen, the ad should include the appropriate contact information to reach the sales team and an email address to reach the right person with any other inquiries.

◼ *Consumer Advertising.* Of course a full-page ad in a major newspaper or magazine may seem ideal, but if there isn't a huge budget for advertising and the author isn't very well-known, one ad won't have that much of an impact. Sometimes the best way to think about consumer advertising is to think small. Are there newspapers, newsletters, or magazines devoted to the book's subject areas?

Once a list of publications has been compiled, visit their websites. Almost all publications provide editorial calendars and details about their advertising programs. A few hours of research might unearth a wealth of marketing opportunities. Also, the publication may sell related items, including books, on their website. This could be an excellent opportunity for additional sales.

If the publication has a book review section, advertising dollars could be saved by getting coverage in a review instead. But still, reaching 30,000 targeted readers who subscribe to a publication that addresses their interests might be worth the expense. If ad rates are prohibitive, perhaps the publication has mailing lists that might be appropriate for a direct mail campaign.

■ **Vendor-specific advertising.** There are also opportunities for specialized advertising through the vendors themselves that are worth pursuing. For instance, often online retailers offer special promotions, such as Amazon's featured ebook "Daily Deal" with a price reduction. These types of deals are selected by editors, so the title must be submitted according to their schedule. A distributor should be aware of these dates, but generally Amazon works in quarters.

Another opportunity that is highly competitive but yields great rewards is a co-op placement in bookstores. This is the table-top or window placement that catches the consumer's eye when they walk in the door. Titles must be nominated for these promoting which are available for a fee, which can run from $1,200 to $30,000, and even up to $50,000 depending on placement. An upside to this fee is that bookstores have to order a significant amount of stock in order to back-up the table placement.

Yet another option is banner ads on vendors' websites. Usually information about purchasing a banner ad can be found on the website itself. The design of these ads is important, and it's best to keep them simple with limited, straightforward copy and a large image of the book or brand.

Trade shows

Many independent publishers feel they do not belong at Book Expo America (BEA). They think that the show belongs to the big boys, that it is way too expensive, and that there is nothing tangible to be gained from it. Well, all of this is true in a way, but our experience with the show tends to override the negatives in some very important ways. We believe that BEA is one of the most important events on the publishing calendar.

Publishing is a networking business, and BEA has become a wonderful networking show. It is a great time and place to discover new markets, new sales opportunities, and make new friends. It can be an excellent source of information on what the competition is doing, and it is a great source of promotion ideas. When possible, attend some lectures and events to learn more about the issues and opportunities in publishing today.

BEA has grown beyond the bookstore market. A wide variety of publishers and groups involved in domestic and foreign rights opportunities now exhibit at BEA. This is an excellent opportunity to think about the rights potential of new titles. Plus, major network show producers, reviewers, and other members of the press can be found visiting the exhibits.

Consider attending the parties and events after the show as well. Many publishers and publishing organizations host events, and those can be a great way to meet people and network in a more intimate environment than at the show.

Show Booths

If working with a distributor, they may offer a small booth in their larger stand. This will make it easy to find press and help gain foot traffic, as most distributors put significant resources into advertising their presence at the shows. If that is not a possibility, individual booths can be reserved directly from the show. Renting a booth tends to be expensive, so it might not make sense to take a booth without at least a couple titles or one huge title worth promoting.

Advertising in Show Publications

This can be a great way to promote a title or list. The *PW Show Daily* publication is given away for free to everyone who attends the show, and visitors tend to consult it early in the day. It often helps inform how show visitors spend their time at the show, so using it to promote an author signing is a great way to get a crowd. There might also be show producers, bloggers, audio book publishers, and other people who see the book and are interested in working with the author or publisher.

Awards

Awards can help with additional sales and also future books. Consider awards from the book community as well as those offered by organizations and associations focused on the subject. And when a book garners that award, inform the sales staff and send out a press release. Many reviewers will take a second look if they think they missed something. There are, of course, the big awards like the Pulitzer, the National Book Award, etc., but there are many smaller awards that can also help win the book some attention. Some worth considering include The Nautilus Award, Independent Book Publisher Awards, Next Generation Indie Book Awards, and Books for a Better Life

Awards. If the book is geared toward children, consider Mom's Choice Awards, Parents' Choice Awards, or the Cybils. If it is a cookbook, consider the IACP and James Beard awards. Of course, just a little research will result in many other options.

Every award has specific deadlines and submissions instructions, so be sure to keep abreast of the deadlines. Also, every award requires an entry fee, so it is a good idea to re-search the awards and their past winners fully to decide where the book has the best chance of winning recognition.

Keeping Sales Reps Informed

In order to maximize the efficiency of all marketing efforts, the sales reps need to be informed every step of the way. If an author appearance on a major television show is scheduled, the reps should know as soon as it's confirmed so that all the sales outlets will have enough books on hand. Marketing ef-forts are worthless if people are convinced to buy the book but the book is unavailable.

A good rule of thumb during the peak of marketing efforts is to keep a running list of media outlets interested and confirmed, and then send a weekly update highlighting this information to all of the sales reps. The circulation of the publications or popularity of the shows should be included, especially if they are not well known. The reps may not have heard of some smaller regional magazines, but if they have a 30,000 circulation, then it's worth telling the reps.

Rights

. . . .

There are many rights associated with a book other than the right to publish it in hardcover, paperback, and ebook formats. Some of them are listed below with brief descriptions. Major publishing houses have entire departments dedicated to selling and managing these rights, which can be very lucrative for the right title.

Domestic

- **Book Club**. There are numerous book club organizations which sell discounted books to their subscribers. Typically, these organizations license the rights to produce inexpensive versions of the books from the publisher and provide an advance against a small royalty for copies sold.

- **Large Print.** For very popular books, publishers will sometimes produce a large print version for people with impaired vision or who prefer to read a larger-print book. There are some companies that specialize in these editions.

- **Audio.** There are numerous companies that produce audio editions of books. Some still produce tapes or CDs, but more often, they produce digital versions for download. For popular books, they might buy the rights by providing an advance against royalties, then produce and distribute the audio book through their channels. Sometimes they request that the author record the book him or herself, but other times, they will use their own vocal talent.

- **Movie.** Film rights can be very lucrative if optioned or purchased. Way more books are optioned for film than are ever bought or made into movies. If a movie version of a book is made, that will typically give the book new life.

- **TV.** Similar to above.

International

- **Agents.** One way to sell foreign rights for titles is to use an agent. Agents tend to specialize in representing titles into a specific market or markets, such as Germany, or the Spanish-language market. If a relationship with an agent is formed, they might want to represent the publisher's titles exclusively to that market. The publisher will send them information about their upcoming titles, including samples when requested, and they will try to interest publishers in their markets in buying the rights to publish the book in their language and market. Agents typically receive a percentage of the advance and royalties in exchange for this, which varies depending on the specific agreement with them.

■ **Scouts.** Scouts are typically kept on retainer by publishers, who want them to keep an eye out in the scout's local market for books that might have appeal in the publisher's market. If a relationship is built with a scout, they will look at the publisher's list and might request samples, and will pass on any interesting titles to their publishing clients in other markets.

■ **Foreign Rights Fairs.** Each year, there are many rights fairs all over the world where publishers and agents meet each other to discuss partnerships and the sales of foreign rights for their titles. The largest of these are the Frankfurt Book Fair in Germany each October, and the London Book Fair in April. There is also a children's books-oriented fair in Bologna which takes place in March, and a South American fair in Guadalajara that happens in November. This is a great place to build relationships with agents, scouts, and publishers.

■ *English.* Some publishers might want to buy the rights to publish titles in the English language. This typically does not preclude a sale in a foreign language in that territory, but be clear about what rights are being licensed in the contract.

■ *Translations.* Foreign publishers might want to buy the rights to publish titles in their language in their local market. There is typically a long submission process before reaching the contract stage, and a lag time between signed contract and publication while they translate the book and make all the other publishing arrangements required to publish a book in any market. Different types of books do better in different countries, and just like in the United States, different publishers have different areas of interest. This can be a lucrative avenue to pursue if a publisher has books in subject areas that are of interest to foreign publishers. Some markets are easier to sell directly, and others will probably require a foreign agent unless a member of the company has a lot of experience selling rights and/or speaks the language.

Catalog

If the publisher has multiple titles, then a foreign rights catalog or rights list is absolutely necessary for any foreign rights fairs and domestic trade shows. The catalog should include the cover image, a short description of the book and the author, and any noteworthy sales points. But the most important information is the book's data, including its genre, specs (hardcover or paperback, trim size, number of pages), ISBN, price, and rights information. Be sure to include any contact information in the catalog as well. The publisher's name, website, and address, as well as the information on how to contact the distributor are necessary.

In this age of technology, many choose to forego printing their catalog, but design it for the internet instead. This is cheaper than budgeting for printing costs, and it is also easily sent through email. This way, the entire file can be emailed to anyone in a meeting on the spot.

Finance

....

Publishing economics are very different than the economics of other businesses. The first major difference is that most books sold to the book trade are actually "sold" on consignment, and paid for by accounts several months later. Books can actually be returned before the payment is due, so publishers must plan carefully and make sure not to spend money before it actually comes in. Print books tend to be sold to the book trade at approximately a 50% discount off the cover price. Some specialty accounts require deeper discounts, though many of them will purchase the books non-returnable, which is advantageous.

When the individual is paid for book sales will depend a lot on what the specific distribution solutions are. Distributors will tell their clients how frequently and on what schedule they will pay them. If books are distributed directly, the author should note when each account will pay. Traditional publishers tend to pay semi-annually and to hold some money in reserve in case they receive too many returns from bookstores.

20 Financial Tips for Independent Publishers

1. If you run a small independent company, do not try to imitate the financial customs and procedures of the traditional publishers. You exist in two separate universes and the only thread that ties you together is that your product is called a book.

2. If the traditional publisher is Goliath, you must be David to survive. David used ingenuity and agility to beat the giant and you can do the same.

3. If you are starting your own company and you have limited capital at your disposal, outsource every activity possible. That way, you will only be paying for time and services as you need them.

4. Publishing is a team sport, and before you have printed one copy of a single book, you should have assembled your entire team (hopefully as outsources). Assembling a team is difficult, but it is critical to have all the people you need for the whole publishing process on the same page before the book is launched.

5. Not every author is expecting a royalty advance, especially if you are a smaller publisher. There are many creative ways of paying an author fairly, including doing a joint venture with him or her. This means sharing the costs and sharing the income.

6. You may not be able to negotiate perfect payment terms (ie, the time you will have to pay the full balance of your

bill) with your printer for your first title, but once you have published and need to reprint, be sure to ask for better payment terms. You may need to persist, but that persistence will pay off in time.

7. There is nothing wrong with starting out on a POD or "short run" basis. It is easy to tie up your money in slow-selling inventory, which has undermined many smaller publishers. Print what you need, and then reprint as you need. POD and short-run printing can have a major positive impact on your use of cash.

8. Books are returnable, which means you have to pay the bookseller or wholesaler back if books are returned. It is important to reserve cash for future returns, because books will come back as surely as the sun rises in the East.

9. If you have a sales force, be sure to ask questions and stay involved in the process. If they are overselling, you are responsible for the cost of the printed books, and printing too many will create a cash drain.

10. Take time to try to understand how distribution works financially. Distribution is an important component, but if you do not know how it really works, you may find that too many of your dollars are going into unnecessary activities. For example, be precise in following shipping instructions to the distributor's warehouse. Extra processing charges such as stickering can mount up quickly. Also, receiving problems at the warehouse can delay shipments, which will cost you sales.

11. Special sales channels often buy books non-returnable at a higher discount. This is an attractive option because you are eliminating the cost of processing returns and creating guaranteed sales.

12. Do not overspend on advertising and other costly marketing activities. For smaller publishers, marketing should follow success, not try to create it. This is a real challenge because we would like to believe that our advertising or publicity will turn the tide in our favor. Costly marketing does make sense if you are Pepsi or Coca-Cola, but most books do not warrant even a tiny fraction of what the big marketers spend on their branded products.

13. Nothing creates positive cash flow faster than a successful book. Many slow-moving titles will do the reverse; these books will eat cash flow and empty your pockets.

14. If a book has stopped selling and inventory is sitting in your warehouse, it makes financial sense to act quickly and remainder the excess inventory. Otherwise your money is tied up in slow-moving books and you may be incurring storage fees.

15. Make sure you have a clause in your author contract that allows you to participate in the revenue if a larger publisher comes along and offers to publish the book. This happens more frequently than you might think.

16. If you have published a successful book and you have money in the bank, do not rush into your next book and assume it will be another bestseller. Take your

time and choose well.

17. If you have a payroll, use a payroll service such as ADP. Their fees are small, and they eliminate a great deal of headache. More importantly, they make sure your payroll taxes are being paid on time.

18. For smaller publishers (and larger ones, for that matter) cash is king. You need to make provisions for those times when cash flow is not covering your operating costs.

19. If you can get a loan, shop around for the most favorable terms.

20. Have a good accounting system in place, so you can track every aspect of your business.

Success Stories

Market, Market, Market

by Steve Harrison

Robert Kiyosaki is no overnight sensation. Many people first heard of his bestselling book *Rich Dad, Poor Dad: What the Rich Teach Their Kids About Money — That the Poor and Middle Class Do Not!* when he appeared on *Oprah* a couple of years ago. The book is the story of Kiyosaki's "two dads" and what each taught him about money. The Rich Dad was Kiyosaki's best friend's father, and the person most responsible for teaching him what the rich know about managing money. Kiyosaki's Poor Dad, his own father, was a government worker who struggled with his finances his entire life. Before that big break, Kiyosaki had put in years of practice learning how to sell himself and his message quickly and effectively. He honed his skills on radio programs, TV programs, and by presenting on stage. As Kiyosaki's Rich Dad said, "If you want to be successful in business, you must learn how to sell."

While *Rich Dad, Poor Dad* is probably his best-known title (10 million copies in print, translated into almost 35 languages), Kiyosaki has slowly built an information empire with other titles that focus on a variety of specific economic concepts, as well as board games, audio and videotape series, and a line of Rich Dad Advisor products. Here are some strategies that Kiyosaki used to build his empire:

- **_Create controversy._** You might think that part of becoming a bestselling author involves cultivating an adoring public. But that's not the way Kiyosaki sees it. In fact, he says that if you're doing your job right, only about 33% of the public is going to love you, with the other two-thirds split evenly between hating you and being indifferent. The reason is because one of the keys to success is controversy—and that is necessarily going to mean ruffling some feathers and making some people downright antagonistic to your message. But controversy makes for a good story, good stories attract media attention, and media attention sells books.

- **_Kill the sacred cow._** How do you go about creating the kind of controversy that grabs the media's attention? Take a generally accepted belief and challenge it. For example, while most homeowners view their house as an asset, Kiyosaki argues just the opposite. In his Rich Dad's world, anything (like your house) that doesn't produce income and that requires you to make payments on it every month can only be considered a liability. As you can imagine, there are plenty of people who didn't like hearing that about the biggest investment of their lives. As Kiyosaki puts it, marketing is like "drawing a line in the sand"—people are either going to agree with what you're saying or they won't. But either way, it's going to attract attention.

- *Make it simple.* In a nutshell, the harder you make it for people to understand the message, the less likely they are to want to buy your book. Kiyosaki's forte is taking the complicated and making it simple. (Most people do just the opposite). Kiyosaki has found that this also makes your message more appealing to the media. If you can't convey the essence of your topic and your most intriguing points in just a few seconds, most people aren't going to wait around to figure out what you're trying to say. And remember, the media loves sound bites.

- *Appeal to a person's spirit.* Kiyosaki's message is powerful for a variety of reasons, not the least of which is the fact that it appeals to one of the most deep-seated desires of most of us: to be financially independent. Kiyosaki has often said, "It's not about making money, it's about being free." It's obvious Kiyosaki has hit an international chord with *Rich Dad, Poor Dad*, making the bestseller lists not only in the United States but also in Japan, China, Korea, Taiwan, Singapore, Indonesia, South Africa, etc.

- *Focus just as much on your marketing as on your writing.* Kiyosaki stresses that he isn't a best writing author, he's a bestselling author. In fact, Kiyosaki doesn't consider himself a particularly talented writer at all. But what he can do is sell. In his youth, Kiyosaki took a job hawking copiers to overcome his fear of selling. It's a skill that pays off to this day. Think about what you do to market your books—you sell yourself to the media, to bookstores, to reviewers, to producers and so on. Knowing how to write is one piece of the puzzle, but knowing how to sell and market your message may be even more important.

- **Be ready for Oprah's call.** According to Kiyosaki, about 99% of authors aren't ready for the dream phone call from one of Oprah's producers. As a result, even a guest spot on one of the most widely watched TV shows in America won't catapult them to bestseller status. The only way to get ready for that call is to practice your media skills, your presentation skills, and how to get your message across most effectively. Kiyosaki has done hundreds of radio and TV interviews (many of which were a result of ads he placed in *Radio-TV Interview Report*, the magazine producers read to find guests) and spoke to live audiences throughout the world in preparation for the day when he got his shot on *Oprah*. That chance came when Kiyosaki was on vacation in the Australian outback on a hunting expedition. After getting the call, he immediately hopped on a plane and flew directly to Chicago for the appearance. Because of the time he spent practicing and his willingness to go the extra mile (or extra few thousand miles, in this case) Kiyosaki attributes selling a million copies of his book to his first *Oprah* appearance.

- **Create high-profit spin-offs.** It's much, much easier (and cheaper for you) if a single customer buys several of your products instead of you constantly recruiting new customers to buy just one product. In other words, if someone buys your $19.95 book and likes it, there's a good chance they'll be interested in your $99.95 audiotape set, or your $199.95 videotape set. Kiyosaki is a believer in this system and created his spin-offs (also known as back-end products) before he ever wrote his book. Essentially, he wrote his book *Rich Dad, Poor Dad* to help him sell a $195 game called CASHFLOW® 101. Don't stop with just one product. If people are responding to your message then why not offer them additional products that give them more information while simultaneously increasing your profit margin?

- **Zero in on niche markets.** When Kiyosaki learned that multi-level marketing companies (mlms) were buying his books and encouraging their associates to read them, he contacted various MLM companies and asked them what they wanted. As a result, he wrote an entire book for them, titled *The Business School for People Who Like Helping People* and sold hundreds of thousands of copies just to various mlms. This is taking the concept of the "special report" several steps further. If you can identify a niche market that would benefit from a specialized version of your book, why not create something tailored just for them? It might be a booklet, a training manual, a tape series or, if the market is big enough like it was for Kiyosaki, an entirely new book. All of Kiyosaki's books include ads at the back for higher-priced games and audio tapes, which range in price from $149 to $295. Many book buyers purchase one or more of these "back-end" products—sales which are very profitable because there's almost no advertising cost.

- **_Build a brand._** The Rich Dad brand is, if not a household name, at least known by enough people that Kiyosaki has been able to expand on his initial product line to offer specialized titles on the subjects of real-estate investing, sales, and tax strategies written by other authors but published under the "Rich Dad" umbrella (the Rich Dad Advisor Series). Like all brands, these products are all instantly recognizable as being part of the same family. Thus, if you liked what Kiyosaki had to say in _Rich Dad, Poor Dad_, chances are you'll be interested in these other topics.

For more information about Robert Kiyosaki, _Rich Dad, Poor Dad_, or any of his other products, visit www.richdad.com. Steve Harrison is the cocreator of BestsellerBlueprint.com with Jack Canfield and the publisher of _Radio-TV Interview Report_, the magazine producers read to find guests.

A Journey through the Grassroots:
The Story Behind the Twelve Gifts of Birth

by Charlene Costanzo

One morning in 1987, when my daughters were teenagers nearing high school graduation, I woke with shock. My children were about to leave home; the most critical years of their development were over; and I was just beginning to understand that unconditional love is the most important thing I could give them. With hindsight, I wished I had done some things differently.

Weeks later, once again I woke one day with strong emotion. This time it was a feeling of euphoria. In the sleep state, I had been in a place where I heard about twelve gifts. I remembered a few of them: Strength, Courage, Beauty, Compassion, Joy; and I recalled a repeated phrase: May you, May you, May you, with what felt like a bestowing of blessings. As I moved into wakefulness, the details of a dream evaporated. Holding on to wisps of it, I wrote a message and fashioned it into a booklet titled *Welcome to the World: The Twelve Gifts of Birth.* It was what I wished I had whispered in my babies' ears and said often as they grew. It told them they were born with gifts. Gentle wishes suggested how to use each gift to live well. I regretted that I had not articulated the message earlier and used it to guide my daughters. But I was just beginning to comprehend it myself.

I felt strongly that all children, not just my own, deserve to hear that they are worthy and gifted. I wanted to see *The Twelve Gifts of Birth* published. With high hopes, I prepared submission packages. After the twentieth rejection, I decided to give up, not on publishing altogether, but on selling *The Twelve Gifts of Birth* to an established publisher. I resolved to publish it myself someday. For years someday was a vague, elusive time in the future. In 1995, I became increasingly disturbed by news stories of abused children. I realized that the message of *The Twelve Gifts of Birth* held potential to help in a small way, and my resolve strengthened. But still I said someday.

A year later my mother's health deteriorated. Sitting in her quiet hospital room one afternoon, I heard a voice within me say "What you do with your time and talent is critically important. Pay attention." I knew immediately what the admonition to pay attention meant. It was time to embrace someday and act upon what was calling me—my book.

My mother died a month later. As soon as I could complete existing projects and fulfill commitments, I told my boss I was leaving recruiting to become a publisher. He encouraged me to follow my dream someday but "not yet," rationalizing that I probably needed a lot more cash than I had to start a business. I tried to conceal the fear and doubt I was feeling in that moment. I knew that, in a way, he was right. I had a nest egg of only $5,000. Still, I decided someday had arrived.

So I left a secure job and became a student of the small press industry, joining organizations like Arizona Book Publishing Association and Publisher's Marketing Association. I attended seminars and read everything I could about self-publishing. I conducted market research and gathered feedback on my little book from local booksellers and gift store owners. I went to Book Expo to find a distributor.

During the entire time I was learning and preparing *The Twelve Gifts of Birth* for publication, I experienced firsthand that miracles do happen when we follow our bliss in the spirit of service. When work is a labor of love, doors open. That was a premise and a promise that I had heard from many sources. And, although I believed it, never before had I acted as if it were true.

It took a year and half of full-time work and $50,000 to bring the richly-illustrated gift book into reality. *The Twelve Gifts of Birth* was released in September 1998, on National KidsDay®, a day intended to recognize the dignity of all children. In unexpected and surprising ways, all the resources that I needed along the way, financial and otherwise, appeared in perfect time. There were times when the steps I took seemed wrong or unnecessary, but later I saw how each "false" step became a stepping stone.

Months before printed books arrived, I sent announcement letters to friends and family. Their orders for multiple copies gave me much moral and some financial support. Twice that summer, my husband, Frank, and I packed up our Jeep with booth equipment and drove from our home in Phoenix to trade shows in the Midwest. We stood for days at gift shows in

Denver and Chicago, offering everyone who passed our booth a card that contained the text of *The Twelve Gifts of Birth*. We asked buyers to read the short, 500-word message when they had some down time. Some people came back within a few minutes, some, a few hours; some, the next day. Many who returned came with moist eyes. But everyone who returned to our booth placed an order for a product yet to be printed.

When our first shipment of 5,000 books arrived, we filled orders. Within two weeks, we started receiving re-orders from gift stores—doubling, tripling, even quadrupling their initial orders. Within a few months we ordered a second, larger printing of 10,000 books.

I had anticipated that the book would do well, but the market's response surpassed my expectations. Many people wrote to say that the message expressed what they yearned to tell their children. Others shared how the book affected them. The first letter I received said, "I am seventy-two years old and have spent years of my life in therapy. I grew up believing that I was worthy only if I accomplished my goals and made a lot of money. My mind and heart have been healed by these twelve gifts. I realize that I live by them today but we both know they have been mine all along."

When I visited local schools and shelters and saw first-hand how eyes brighten when children hear the story, I wished I could do that throughout the country. But that seemed like an impossible dream.

One Saturday afternoon, Frank and I saw an advertisement for a "colossal RV sale" and decided to take a look. After stepping in and out of a few models, we started to act like children playing, sitting in the driver and passenger seats and imagining new vistas and signs welcoming us to states we had not yet visited. After a while, we became quiet, explored models on our own, and looked at prices. On the way home, I said, "I have a crazy idea." Frank said, "Maybe it's not so crazy." We mused over the possibilities of giving up our home, living in a motor home, and Frank taking a sabbatical from consulting. I could read and discuss the message with thousands of children, promote the book, and we could see the country.

The seemingly impossible dream became plausible when a special sales company called to negotiate a large order and ended up purchasing 225,000 copies. Although they paid only a small amount per book over print costs, it financed our trip and allowed Frank to leave his work for a year and focus fully what was fast becoming our mission.

Before buying a motor home, I called a bestselling author who had used one to promote his book. His advice to me was "Don't do it! Imagine your house in an earthquake every day. That is what it sometimes feels like when you are traveling down the highway."

I then called the president of a small press company who had also used a motor home to market a bestseller. He offered some encouragement but counseled me that even a regional tour takes an immense amount of planning, coordination, and follow-up. He had a whole staff working on it. Did I?

Despite the cautions, we went ahead and moved from 2,500 square feet of living space into 250. On a sweltering summer Sunday in July 1999, we merged on I-10 in Phoenix and began a one-year journey throughout the U.S. Frank gripped the wheel with intense focus while I watched the white lines. On both sides of our vehicle the lines seemed dangerously close, too easy to cross. In setting out on this mission, had we crossed a line? I wondered.

After a while our tense muscles eased a bit. We even started to sing until suddenly we heard a pop, felt a jarring shift, and smelled ruptured rubber. My stomach clenched. A flat tire at forty miles into a 40,000 mile trip? Are we making a big mistake? Maybe that author was right.

In many ways both the author and publisher were right. There were many challenges. The balancing jacks came down while we were driving. Low clearance bridges forced detours. On our way to Salt Lake City, on the day the first ever-recorded tornado hit the city, high winds ripped away one of our awnings. Pipes froze during a cold night in West Virginia. There were many challenges with email, regular mail and telephone communication. We often climbed to the roof for cell phone connection. Water leaked through the roof onto our computer during a heavy rainstorm and destroyed data. Forwarded snail mail sometimes got lost.

Creating a schedule was hard; following it was harder. Days were long. TV interviews, when I could get them, were on early morning shows. In late morning and early afternoon, we visited schools and shelters. Bookstore events started at 7:00 PM. We often didn't get situated on a site, hooked up, and in bed until very late. Then, all too often, the roar, whistle, and thundering vibration of a nearby train caused a sleepless night. Fortunately, we were safe and could usually laugh at the adventure of it all. Always, the positives outweighed the negatives. Many nights, when we were able to camp away from populated areas, we gazed at the star-studded sky and pondered our place in it all. We appreciated the diverse and magnificent American landscape as we drove from place to place, crossing mountains, rivers, plains, and prairies. We saw the sun sparkle on the Pacific, the Atlantic, and the Gulf of Mexico.

During the tour I became more aware both of the power within the human spirit and of human suffering. Every day, in addition to talking about the gifts, people disclosed their own struggles. Some stories were volunteered during group presentations, others were confided when I signed books. I am forever grateful and enriched by all the shared stories.

During that year, nearly 300,000 copies of *The Twelve Gifts of Birth* were sold; the book received attention in *Publishers Weekly* and it was recommended by Book Sense. The Twelve Gifts message was licensed for use on a poster and a baby blanket. In July 2000, on the very last day of the tour, I received a call from an agent, offering to help me sell rights to a large publisher.

In 2001, *The Twelve Gifts of Birth* was re-released through HarperCollins Publishers in both English and Spanish, and has been followed by *The Twelve Gifts for Healing* and *The Twelve Gifts in Marriage*. *The Twelve Gifts of Birth* is also available in Japanese. The book continues to sell well and is being used in many ways by educators, therapists, clergy, and social workers. Several hospitals have decorated their birthing center walls with the message of *The Twelve Gifts of Birth*. A short film based on the book is being created for educational and inspirational use. For more information, visit

www.thetwelvegifts.com.

Blind Faith and Serendipity: One Author's Unlikely Journey from Self-Publishing to the Viking Frontlist

by Philip Beard

T he story of how *Dear Zoe* found its way to Viking is one I still have trouble believing. If you have ever doubted the combined powers of blind persistence and serendipity, then read on.

After practicing law full-time for eleven years, I began work on my first novel, billing just enough hours from home to make family grocery money. Fueled mostly by fear, I finished it in nine months, and a year later secured a wonderful agent, Jane Dystel, to represent it. I was still naïve enough to believe that agents were magic, that a book deal was now imminent, and that the transition from my old career to my new one was complete. Six months and twenty-seven rejection letters later, *The Love Number* went back in the drawer. Fortunately, I had followed Jane's advice and was already halfway through a first draft of a second novel, and by January 2003, *Dear Zoe* was ready for submission.

After the first six rejection letters arrived, I was advised by more than one person that I should change the point of view before submitting to any more publishers—that the epistolary format of *Dear Zoe* took away from the intimacy between narrator and reader and should be re-thought. I had resisted that advice for months, but, having already had one novel rejected by every major house in New York, I was willing to do just about anything to avoid the same fate for the second. I spent a month revising the novel to standard first person, changed the title to *Z*, then sat and cried when I sent it off that way.

The change didn't help. Three months later, the last of the twenty-eight rejection letters arrived. We came close more than once (I will always be indebted to Reagan Arthur at Little, Brown for her encouragement and for championing *Z* at that fine house), but in the end I was faced with the prospect of starting work on a third novel without any faith that it would find a home. I couldn't do it. Knowing that others had found success with their third or fourth books didn't help. I felt lost, directionless, paralyzed by the first real failure of my life. I couldn't picture myself going back to the practice of law full-time, yet three attempts to start a new novel went nowhere. I spent the spring and summer performing mindless tasks: I worked for my younger brother (the ultimate humiliation), finishing the new wood paneling in his basement, getting slightly looped on polyurethane; I went to the gym; got the yard in shape; I spent too much time watching the war in Iraq on CNN; I cleaned and alphabetized all eight hundred beer cans from the childhood collection that had been rusting in my parents' attic for twenty-five years; I wore out two pairs of sneakers walking the dog. Then I saw an article in the *New York Times* about self-publishing and decided to take back control of my new career.

I spent the next six months treating the publication of *Dear Zoe* as my full-time job. I went back to the earlier version of the manuscript—restoring both the original title and the original point of view —and read every text on self-publishing I could find. I formed Van Buren Books as a Pennsylvania LLC, solicited competing bids from small printers who took the time to teach me the difference between smythe sewn and adhesive case bindings, gloss and lay-flat matte lamination, headbands, footbands, endsheets, and binder boards. I found a cover designer (Amy King), a national distributor willing to take a chance on the book (Midpoint Trade Books), a tireless, imaginative publicist (Maryglenn McCombs), and I sent the manuscript to every published writer I had ever met (and some I hadn't) asking them to read *Dear Zoe* and consider providing a blurb for the back cover.

The key to finding all of these crucial contributors was, quite simply, not being afraid to ask. I knew my chances of success were minuscule, but I was energized by the ability to control every aspect of the process, by creating and following every small lead. For example, I found Amy King by taking fifty of my favorite covers off my shelves, checking the flaps for the designer credits, and stacking each designer in individual piles (you'd be surprised how few cover designers there are in New York). My wife and I agreed that Amy's covers were consistently the strongest, and I called Doubleday the next day looking for her. I was told that Amy no longer worked there, but that her husband was still with Random House. I asked to be transferred to him, and then found myself in New York Publishing Limbo—the secretary's voice mail—leaving a long meandering message about why I was looking for "your boss's wife." Incredibly, Amy King called me the next day. Pregnant with her second child, she had just left Doubleday to open her own design shop and was looking for new clients.

My agent, Jane Dystel, was invaluable during this time as well. I was afraid she was going to caution me that self-publishing would be akin to literary suicide, but she was supportive from the beginning. She put me in touch with a tough publicity veteran, Rick Frishman, who gave me more of his time than I could have hoped for, along with some honest, sage advice that went something like this: "You're insane, you know; but if you insist on doing this, you'll need a distributor." He directed me to Eric Kampmann, President of Midpoint Trade Books, and if Eric initially took me on as a favor to Rick, he gradually became a vocal and active advocate for my novel. Eric, in turn, sent me to Maryglenn, my publicist. I had galleys produced at Express Media in Nashville using Amy King's design, and I settled on Thomson-Shore in Michigan to print 3,000 hardcover books. The project was really moving along nicely, even gathering a little momentum. But to finish the story, I first need to go back.

Just after deciding to self-publish, I was in my favorite independent bookstore, The Aspinwall Bookshop, two blocks from my home. When I was in law school, the proprietor, John Towle, had worked for a Pittsburgh indie bookseller institution, Jay Dantry of Jay's Bookstall, alongside then-Pitt writing student Michael Chabon. I came to know John not just as someone who sold books, but as someone who recommended great books. Completely by chance, when I graduated from law school and moved to Aspinwall, John left Jay's and, after an interim location or two, opened his own one-room shop on my street. When I started writing again, John became the first unbiased barometer of my work.

The day I stopped by to tell John about my self-publishing plans, he told me that his Penguin sales rep, Jason Gobble, was due to stop in later that week, and that Jason was some-one who "has some credibility with the editors at Penguin." I told John that the book had already been rejected by most of the Penguin imprints, but agreed to drop off a copy of the manuscript the next day.

A few months later, John called to tell me that Jason loved *Dear Zoe* and wanted permission to send it to Viking. I agreed but with no expectations. I had already wallpapered my office with rejection letters from New York, and I was cer-tain this was going to be one more. What I was excited about, however, was the possibility of having an influential regional sales rep behind my book. Jason Gobble and I struck up an email friendship, and although he couldn't "officially" repre-sent my book to the independents in his five-state territory, he agreed to distribute my galleys informally to all of his best hand-sellers with a strong recommendation.

Just weeks after sending my manuscript off to Viking,

Jason Gobble was named by *Publishers Weekly* as its Sales Rep of the Year and was featured in a three-page spread. Suddenly, Van Buren Books and *Dear Zoe* had a very influential advocate. Over the course of the next couple of months, I increased my planned print run to 5,000 copies, and Maryglenn and Midpoint both scheduled signings for me at the BookExpo in Chicago in June 2004. I had one hundred galley copies printed for distribution through Jason to booksellers, through Maryglenn to reviewers, and through Midpoint to their national account reps, and Amy King and I finalized the jacket design. During that time, I honestly never gave a thought to the Viking submission.

On March 23, 2004, I was sitting at my computer, corresponding with Amy King on the final jacket layout. The overall design had been set for weeks, but we had been struggling with the logo for Van Buren Books that would appear on the spine. To stay within my publication timeline, we needed to have the final design mechanicals to our printer within a couple of days. At the same time, I would write the largest check of my life to print books I couldn't be sure anyone beyond my Christmas card list would buy. I sent an email to Amy with my final decision on the logo, instructing her to get the mechanicals to the printer by the next day. Then I called Maryglenn, confirmed that we were on schedule, and told her to start sending the galleys out to the advance reviewers. When I clicked back to my in-box, there was an email from the receptionist at my law firm that said the following:

"Clare Ferraro from Viking called and would like you to call her back. She said to say she works with Jason Gobble."

I stared at that message, motionless, for what must have been a full minute. I knew that Clare Ferraro didn't just "work with Jason Gobble," that she was the president of Viking Penguin. And although I couldn't imagine how a call from her could possibly be bad news, it just didn't seem possible that, after four years, a novel of mine was going to find a home in New York on the same day I was finalizing plans to print it myself. Of course, that's exactly what happened. By the end of the day, Jane Dystel had come to an agreement with Viking, and I had notified everyone involved in my self-publishing effort that Van Buren Books was suspending operations. Three weeks later, *Dear Zoe* appeared in the "Hot Deals" column of *Publishers Weekly*. Unbelievable.

Still, I am probably the only writer who ever felt a sense of nostalgia along with the elation of finally being validated by New York. In the process of preparing *Dear Zoe* to go to press, I came to know every player in the chain of production, promotion, and distribution in a way that can never happen at a major publishing house; nor should it. The people at Viking have done more for *Dear Zoe* than I could ever have hoped to do on my own. For the month of its release in April 2005, *Dear Zoe* was both a Book Sense Pick and a Borders "Original Voices" selection. An audio version, as read by actress Cassandra Morris, was released simultaneously by Highbridge Audio and won an Audiofile "Earphones" Award. More recently,

Booklist named *Dear Zoe* one of the Ten Best First Novels of 2005, and it was selected as a Book Sense Summer Paperback for the summer of 2006. And remember that first novel that went into the drawer? Viking purchased that one as well and published *Lost in the Garden* in May 2006.

Fortunately, I have been able to continue my relationship with many of the people I worked with in my self-publishing effort: Amy King was retained by Viking to work on its version of the *Dear Zoe* cover; Maryglenn McCombs still emails me with sage promotional advice; Jason Gobble got to sell the novel he discovered in the tiny Aspinwall Bookshop until he moved on to a new job with Ingram; and John Towle, the owner of that shop and always the first person outside my family to read my work, hosted my first official book signing and has sold more copies of both of my novels than any other bookseller in the country.

The Necessity of Teamwork

By Eric Kampmann

T he real story behind the publication of the notorious O. J. Simpson tell-all, *If I Did It*, has never been told, until now.

Some may remember the storm of controversy surrounding the announcement in November 2006 that HarperCollins intended to publish O. J. Simpson's version of what happened on the night that Ron Goldman and Nicole Simpson were viciously attacked and murdered. The Goldman and Brown families were understandably outraged that O. J. Simpson might make a profit off the death of their loved ones. Enormous public pressure, led by the Goldman and Brown families, turned the story into a hot topic. HarperCollins eventually cancelled the publication of the book in the hopes of containing the damage.

While the cancellation quieted the media frenzy, *If I Did It* did not die. HarperCollins relinquished the rights to publish the book, returning them to O. J. Simpson through a shell corporation he owned. But the Goldman legal team would not rest. Until that point, in 2007, the Goldmans had never been able to collect any of the millions of dollars in damages they had won in a civil suit against O. J. Simpson. He had successfully kept the Browns and Goldmans at bay for a decade through numerous legal maneuvers.

But now O. J.'s luck had run out. The Goldman legal team

pursued the rights to the book through the Florida court system, and won them in a bankruptcy proceeding on July 31st. They were required by the court to "monetize the asset," which simply meant that the Goldmans and their team needed to find a way to get the manuscript successfully published. This is where I entered the picture.

In early August, a literary agent who was friendly with the Goldman family contacted me through David Nelson, the publisher of Beaufort Books at the time, to see if we might be interested in working with the Goldmans to publish *If I Did It*. The only problem, she stated, was that we had less than six weeks to get the job done, since Kim and Fred Goldman were locked into an appearance on *Oprah* on September 13th.

Industry professionals know that it takes a year or more to get most books to market. So the first order of business was to determine whether Beaufort and Midpoint could get the job done in such a short amount of time. We had to review the manuscript, design the interior, design the cover, get an introduction and afterword written, and have the Goldmans write the foreword. In addition to all this, we needed to determine the appropriate print run and get the books printed in time to land in stores by the 13th of September.

To make matters more complicated, I departed for Maine on August 2nd for a weeklong vacation. It was not clear that getting involved with this project was sensible. There were many risks, including the public's apparent distaste for a book written by O. J. Simpson, even if that book included some sensational information. I spoke with many people inside the company and out about the viability of the project. I evaluated time and again the team's capacity to get a very difficult job done in such a short amount of time. I worried about the amount of money needed to get the book launched, and I considered the possibility of receiving negative publicity.

On August 5th, I took a day hike up Mt. Champlain on Mt. Desert Island. As we rested halfway up, I realized that the time to decide had arrived. Maybe it was the serenity of the setting, but the clock was ticking and I needed to either decline the invitation to enter the O. J. Simpson story, or enter it full speed ahead, casting fear and doubt aside. By the time I was off the mountain, I had made the decision to proceed. Behind everything else was my realization that this challenge could be a turning point for both Beaufort and Midpoint. Given the clear benefits that would come with success, I felt I could not turn my back on the opportunity even with the obvious risks. If the Goldmans decided they wanted to work with me, then I would do everything in my power to do exactly as the judge had instructed the Goldmans to do: Monetize the asset.

The contract with Fred and Kim Goldman was signed on August 11th. Following that moment, we were off to the races. Margot Atwell, managing editor at Beaufort at the time, took on the whole editorial management of the book, and Beth Metrick and Pauline Neuwirth of Neuwirth and Associates took over the book's production. Chris Bell, vice president of

Midpoint, managed the sales side.

Margot, Pauline, and Beth worked together almost around the clock to get the text finalized and the interior designed in time. Meanwhile, the Midpoint sales team approached their accounts with the unusual problem of a book hitting three weeks later, but still managed to get strong orders.

We ran into a number of obstacles on the way to publication, but one of the biggest was internal. Fred and Kim Goldman viscerally objected to the title "If I Did It." As far as they were concerned, O. J. did it, and there should be no expression of doubt in the title. On the other hand, the public already knew the title, since the book had received a gigantic amount of publicity over a period of many months. All the major TV producers told us that we needed to keep the original title. It was iconic. What to do? We struggled with this problem for several days, because we wanted to honor Fred and Kim's wishes, but we did not want to sabotage the sales by confusing the public with a new title.

In the end, two people led to the answer. Alison Baker, a friend of my son Alex, suggested we reduce the size of the word "If" and perhaps place the "If" inside the "I" of the title so that to the human eye it would read "I Did It." And it was Pauline Neuwirth who brilliantly executed the design, creating in two short days a book cover that satisfied all parties.

Michael Wright of Garson and Wright Public Relations worked with us to create the most possible impact with the book launch, advising us on when to go public with the information that we were publishing this previously very unpopular book. The campaign got under way with my appearance on several TV shows including *The Today Show*. Michael also booked the Goldmans onto *Dr. Phil* and got other media opportunities for them.

Soon after the announcement of the book's publication, the book flew up to the number one position on both the Amazon and Barnes & Noble bestseller lists. The public clearly wanted to read O. J.'s side of the story. At the same time, a wave of negative press hit. Many did not understand that the Goldman family now owned the book and that they had been instructed by a judge to get it published. Neither did people understand that O. J. wouldn't receive any money. All profits would go to the Goldman and Brown families.

The rest of the story is history. We printed 125,000 copies and sold out immediately. The Goldmans appeared on *Oprah* on September 13th, and at about the same time, O. J. Simpson burst into a hotel room in Las Vegas with a gun, an act that got him enormous publicity and a long sentence of prison time. The book went into a second printing and hit the number-two spot on the *New York Times* Non-Fiction Bestseller List on October 7th.

The decision to publish had nothing to do with the ethics of the situation. The Goldman family owned the book. They were told to publish it, and in the end, I believed I could do a good job publishing it for them. But the project was risky on many levels. We could not afford one instance of Murphy's

Law interfering. Everyone, including Margot Atwell, Chris Bell, and Pauline Neuwirth, was heroic in accomplishing so much in such a short period of time. The team was more than up to the challenge; the risk had been significant but the Beaufort/Midpoint team worked together at the highest level of professionalism. As I look back at all the events surrounding the publication of *If I Did It*, I believe it wasn't the work of one individual that made the difference; it was the teamwork of the whole group that transformed risk into success.

Acknowledgments

· ·

Putting together a book is always a team effort. We've had a fantastic team that helped us put together this one, and we are very grateful for their efforts.

For being there at the beginning and helping to get this whole thing off the ground, Sarah Lucie and Liam Ferguson deserve our deepest thanks. Megan Trank has also been an invaluable part of the process.

For her gorgeous design and incredible patience, much praise goes to Jane Perini of Thunder Mountain Designs. We have Zak Deardoff of Deardoff Industries to thank for our cover design.

For contributing sections and stories, we are grateful to Jen Moschella, James Fischer, Julie Hardison, Steve Harrison, Charlene Costanzo, and Philip Beard.

Additional thanks go to Kerry Wimley, Caroline DeLuca, Lauren Fiorelli, Cindy Peng, Ryan Jenkins, and Rachel Wheeler.

We would also like to thank all the other people who made this book possible, and who make all our books possible.

Additional Resources

....

Agility
Run by PR Newswire, Agility is a subscription-based database of media contacts. Contacts range from bloggers to TV show producers.
agility.prnewswire.com

Amazon.com
Online marketplace where users can find almost anything. Amazon.com has entered the ebook market, releasing its own ereader called "Kindle." Kindles come in various styles and prices. **amazon.com**

Barcode Graphics
Users can easily create a barcode for $10. Once registered, users select the size, input the price and ISBN, and create a barcode. Barcodes can be emailed or downloaded within minutes.
createbarcodes.com/index.aspx

Barnes & Noble
Barnes & Noble has a wide range of books (hardcover to ebooks), electronic newspaper subscriptions, DVDs, music, and gifts. Barnes & Noble has an ereader called "Nook." Nooks come in various styles and prices.
barnesandnoble.com

The Book Cover Archive
A photo database of cover designs and contact information for designers. **bookcoverarchive.com**

Bookjobs.com
Provides job and internship postings for various publishing-related positions. **bookjobs.com**

Bowker Identifier Services
This is the official source for ISBNs in the United States. Users can buy single ISBNs or sets of 10, 100, or 1000 ISBNs. **myidentifiers.com**

Bowker: U.S. ISBN Agency
United States ISBN Bowker Agency's website. Provides the official sources for purchasing ISBNs, barcodes, and SANs (Standard Address Number). Also provides information for converting 10-digit ISBNs to 13-digit ISBNs. **isbn.org**

Cataloging in Publication Program
Run by the Library of Congress, publishers submit applications for Cataloging in Publication data (CIP data). This data is then placed on the copyright page. The data is primarily used by librarians and booksellers when selecting and cataloging their books. **loc.gov/publish/cip/**

Cision
Cision is a subscription-based publicity contact database for print and online media, similar to Agility. **us.cision.com**

Createspace.com
Owned by Amazon.com, CreateSpace provides an on-demand service for books, CDs, and DVDs. For authors interested in self-publishing, CreateSpace takes care of the manufacturing and shipping. There are free tools as well as professional services for authors who need help creating a book's interior and cover design. **createspace.com**

Facebook

A free social networking site that allows personal pages, fan pages (used by business, authors, or celebrities), or groups (common-interest groups, companies, or schools). Users can connect, comment, "like," and share information easily with "friends" they have accepted. **facebook.com**

Flickr

A photo-sharing site run by Yahoo! Photos can be marked as public or private, as well as shared with friends through social media. Free and paid accounts are available. **flickr.com**

Goodreads

A free site for book recommendations and for connecting with readers. They offer a publisher program as well as an author program.
goodreads.com

Google+

Owned by Google, this free social networking site is similar to Facebook. Users can connect with friends, colleagues, and fans using "circles" to organize contacts. **plus.google.com**

Gotham Ghostwriters

A New York City-based full-service writing firm.
gothamghostwriters.com

Ingram ipage

Used by publishers and booksellers, Ingram ipage offers title and ordering information, stock status, and publishing related news. This service is free for Ingram customers. **ipage.ingramcontent.com**

LibraryThing

Online cataloging service for the general public. Allows users to catalog up to 200 books for free. Paid accounts are available.
librarything.com

LinkedIn

A free networking site for professionals to post profiles, resumes, and job openings. A great way to connect with industry colleagues. **linkedin.com**

Literary Market Place™

A directory of American and Canadian book publishing resources. A great place to find literary agents, publishers, suppliers, printers, and more. There is a print version as well as an electronic version. A subscription is required. **literarymarketplace.com**

Mediabistro

Provides anyone who works with or creates content a place to share resources, find jobs and projects, and display their work. **mediabistro.com**

Overstock.com

An online retailer that has bargain prices. **overstock.com**

Pinterest

Pinterest allows users to share and organize pictures and ideas on virtual pinboards. Boards are shared with the rest of the Pinterest community, allowing users to connect through shared pins and interests. This is a free site. **pinterest.com**

Publishers Marketplace

A unique database that allows publishing professionals to connect and work electronically. This is a service of Publishers Lunch, an eNewsletter read by over 40,000 professionals each day.
publishersmarketplace.com

PW Daily

Publishers Weekly offers six different free eNewsletters. PW Daily reports on the important stories within the book publishing industry. Stories include signed deals, sales information, personnel changes, employment, and author appearances. **publishersweekly.com**

Spotify
An online music service connected to Facebook that allows users to share and listen to music. Three types of accounts are available, two with a monthly fee and one for free. Options vary depending on which account has been selected. **spotify.com**

Twitter
A free social networking site where users share information in posts of 140 characters or fewer. **twitter.com**

Vocus
A cloud-based publicity software designed for businesses to reach buyers using social networks. A subscription is required. **vocus.com**

Index

Authors

. . . .

Eric Kampmann is currently the President and CEO of Midpoint Trade Books, a sales, marketing, and distribution company that currently represents over 150 independent book publishers. Eric began his career in book publishing as a sales rep at the Viking Press in 1970. He became Assistant Sales Manager there and then moved on to St. Martin's Press as Director of Sales. In 1977, he moved to Simon & Schuster as National Sales Manager, then to VP and Director of Sales.

Before launching Midpoint in 1996, Eric built Kampmann & Company into one of the top distribution companies for independent publishers.

Eric is the author of numerous books: *The Book Publisher's Handbook, Awakenings, Trail Thoughts,* and *Signposts.* He has taught publishing courses at Harvard, Columbia, Hofstra, and New York University. Eric has appeared on *The Today Show*, Fox News, CNN, The BBC, and been featured in publications such as *The New York Times*, *The Wall Street Journal*, the *LA*

Times, The Associated Press, Reuters, Bloomberg, and *Publishers Weekly*. He received his BA from Brown University and a graduate degree from Stony Brook University. He has also been a speaker at many publishing and writers conferences.

Margot Atwell has worked in publishing since she was a student at Smith College, where she founded and edited *Labrys*, a journal of art and literature. Following graduation, she moved to New York to take a job at a literary agency. Margot eventually switched over to the publishing side, and has worked with Beaufort Books for seven years. She has published four national bestsellers in that time. Margot is also a freelance writer, editor, and book reviewer, and has written for publications such as *Publishers Weekly, Publishing Perspectives, Moviefone*, and *Five on Five*. She co-founded and runs Derbylife.com. This is her first book.

THE
INSIDER'S GUIDE
TO
BOOK PUBLISHING
SUCCESS